POVERTY AND THE WELFARE STATE

By B. Seebohm Rowntree and G. R. Lavers
ENGLISH LIFE AND LEISURE: A SOCIAL STUDY

By B. Seebohm Rowntree
POVERTY AND PROGRESS

POVERTY AND THE WELFARE STATE

A third social survey of York dealing only
with economic questions

by

B. SEEBOHM ROWNTREE

and

G. R. LAVERS

LONGMANS, GREEN AND CO
LONDON · NEW YORK · TORONTO

LONGMANS, GREEN AND CO LTD
6 & 7 CLIFFORD STREET LONDON W 1

ALSO AT MELBOURNE AND CAPE TOWN

LONGMANS, GREEN AND CO INC
55 FIFTH AVENUE NEW YORK 3

LONGMANS, GREEN AND CO
215 VICTORIA STREET TORONTO 1

ORIENT LONGMANS LTD.
BOMBAY CALCUTTA MADRAS

First published 1951

Printed and Bound in Great Britain by
ALLDAY LIMITED, BIRMINGHAM 3

AUTHORS' NOTE

The authors gratefully acknowledge the assistance they have received from many individuals in compiling and interpreting the great volume of factual information on which this book is based. In particular they are indebted to:

Miss T. Schulz, PH.D., of the Oxford University Institute of Statistics, and Mr. Stanley Tennant, who gave valuable help in relation to the dietary adopted when establishing the poverty line.

Messrs. L. E. Waddilove and P. J. Pfluger who acted as the authors' representatives and intermediaries in York and smoothed over many difficulties.

Drs. C. B. Crane, M.B., B.S., D.P.H., and F. B. Shevlin, M.B., CH.B., respectively the Medical Officer of Health and School Medical Officer of Health in York, Mr. C. J. Minter, O.B.E., M.I.M. & CY.E., the City Engineer and Architect, and Mr. N. Hancock, M.R.S.I., M.S.I.A., the Chief Sanitary Inspector, all of whom undertook detailed enquiries into matters in their particular spheres.

Miss Joyce Hildreth and Mrs. P. North, the authors' secretaries, who, in addition to their normal duties, made a number of the calculations used in the book, and checked others.

Finally the authors wish to express their deep sense of obligation to all the employers and Trade Union officials whose understanding of the purpose of the book, and friendly co-operation, made it possible for the authors to obtain information about the actual earnings of a very large majority of the chief wage-earners in the houses visited.

B.S.R.
G.R.L.

HIGH WYCOMBE,
June, 1951.

NOTE ON PRICES

As is explained in Chapter 2 of this book, the enquiries about prices and habits of expenditure on which our poverty line is based were made in October, 1950. It has been suggested to us that as prices of many commodities have risen substantially since that date our division of the working-class population between Classes 'A' to 'E' may no longer be accurate. In fact, as we have established by actual checks in a considerable number of cases, taking wage increases into account, the change in the distribution between the Classes is a trifling one.

B.S.R.
G.R.L.

High Wycombe,
June, 1951.

CONTENTS

CHAPTER ONE

PURPOSE AND METHOD OF THE ENQUIRY

The purpose of this book is to throw light on the question of how far the various welfare measures which have come into force since 1936 have succeeded in reducing poverty. It occurred to us that we were peculiarly fortunately placed to answer this question because B. S. Rowntree had made a social survey of York in 1900 and another one in 1936,* so that if we made a social survey of York in 1950 on the same lines as those adopted in 1936, but dealing only with economic questions, we should have an accurate yard-stick for measuring the comparative amount of poverty in the city in those two years.

In 1936 B. S. Rowntree's investigators visited every working-class house in the city where the chief wage-earner was earning not more than £250 a year. After seeking the advice of persons competent to judge what income in 1950 was equivalent to £250 in 1936, we took a figure of £550 and our survey has accordingly been restricted to families where the chief wage-earner (and his wife if she went out to work) received not more than that figure.

B. S. Rowntree's previous social surveys are the only ones that have been based on visits paid to *every* working-class house. In others the sampling method has been adopted. After he had almost finished writing the report of his second social survey of York,

* The results of these surveys were published in his two books, "Poverty: A Study of Town Life" and "Poverty and Progress: A Second Social Survey of York".

it occurred to him that he had the information available to test the margin of error which would result if, instead of investigating every family, he had adopted the sampling method and had based his results on the investigation of various proportions of the households taken at random. Accordingly he arranged the 16,362 schedules in street order and took every tenth one, just as if calling at every tenth house. He compared the results with those obtained from the complete house-to-house investigation. He made similar calculations based on samples of one in twenty, one in thirty, one in forty, and one in fifty.* In view of the information thus gained, we determined that substantially accurate results would be obtained if instead of investigating *every* house, one in ten were investigated. As this decision had to be made before the reliability of the information gained by the investigators could be tested by check visits, we decided to visit one house in every nine, thinking that some of the schedules might have to be discarded because they did not give complete and accurate information. G. R. Lavers called on a number of the houses which had been visited by our investigators and found no cases in which they had furnished inadequate or incorrect information. In fact, the number of schedules it was necessary to discard was insignificant, and thus our results are based on a sample of one in nine working-class households.

A word must here be said about how we chose the streets to be visited by our investigators. We took a list of all the streets in York, and a man who has lived in the city for more than half a century, who knows the city intimately, and has also a wide knowledge of, and sympathy with, our work, marked on our list every street where working-class families live.

---

* Detailed figures showing the result of this investigation are given in "Poverty and Progress," pp.481, *et seq*.

Although our investigators sought no information about the earnings of the householders, or their wives if they went out to work, they obtained information about payments made for board and lodging by other members of the household, whether children or lodgers. We give on pages 4 and 5 a typical schedule to show the kind of information we obtained. Further examples of the information given on the schedules will be found in Chapters 8 and 9.

Before giving detailed information about the investigation that we have made, a few particulars must be given about the population of York and its main industries.

At the time of our investigation, there had been no national census since 1931. The population of the city was estimated by the Medical Officer of Health to have been 89,680 in 1936 when the previous social survey was made, and in 1949 the Medical Officer of Health estimated the population as being 104,600.

There are two main industries in York. The Railway Executive employs about 8,100 men and lads, as compared with 7,800 in 1936. The other main industry is the manufacture of cocoa, chocolate, and general confectionery. In 1936 the number employed was nearly 10,000 and in 1950 it was practically the same. About 4,400 of those employed were males. The number employed in the industry was much higher than this immediately before the war; the subsequent reduction in numbers is due to the shortage of raw materials.

Minimum wages in the Cocoa and Confectionery industry are fixed by a Wages Council, but the two principal firms in York pay wages on the scale agreed upon for the industry by the Joint Industrial Council. These are higher than the Wages Council rates. The

Name of Householder   Mr. XYZ

Street and Number   22 Lake Success Terrace

Rent } £1.2s.9d.
Rates }

Total number of occupants 8 (including lodger)
Number of rooms 6
Bathroom (Yes or No) Yes

Members of Household and status.	Age.	Sex.	Occupation and where employed.	Wage.
Mr. XYZ	57	M	Railway Worker	£5.19s.6d.
Mrs. XYZ	50	F	Housewife	
Daughter	18	F	Packing Dept. of -- & Co	
Daughter	17	F	Packing Dept. of -- & Co	£2. 5s.0d.
Daughter	15	F	Open-Air School. Value of School milk	2s.3d.
Son	9	M	School Family allowances	10s.0d.
Son	8	M	School Value of vegetables grown	2s.6d.
Mr. ABC. (Lodger)	31	M	Bus. Driver Paid by lodger	£1.10s.0d.

Do the children receive free School meals?   No; pay 2s. 6d. each per week

Do the children receive free milk (*a*) at School?   Yes

         (*b*) in holidays?   No

Amount paid by each child in employment for board and lodging   Eldest 25s. a week; Second 20s.

Amount paid by lodgers   30s. a week

Amount received from sub-tenants not boarded.   None

Sums received for:—

    Unemployment Insurance   None

    National Assistance (*i.e.* "Public" Assistance)   None

    Health Insurance   None

    Sick Clubs   None   War Pension   None   Widow's Pension   None

    Old Age Pension (including supplementary)   None

Are all/most/some of vegetables consumed home grown?   Yes – some

GENERAL OBSERVATIONS ON HOUSEHOLD:— A modern council house. The family have not really recovered from four years' continuous unemployment 1934–37. Buying furniture on instalment system (15s.9d.) per week. Complained of high cost of children's clothes and poor quality of shoe leather.

minimum in 1950 was 100s. a week for an adult male
and 69s. for an adult female. A very high proportion
of the workers in the industry are engaged on piece
work, and it was laid down that the earnings of a piece-
worker of average ability shall be not less than 125s.
for an adult male and 86s. 3d. for an adult female.
The two principal firms in the industry work a forty-
four hour week.

Average earnings on the Railway vary, of course,
according to the work on which the men are engaged,
but even the lowest paid adult worker earns sufficient
to keep him above the poverty line.

We think that the following statement made in
"Poverty and Progress" still holds true:

> "On the whole, I think, we may safely assume
> that from the standpoint of the earnings of the
> workers, York holds a position not far from the
> median, among the towns of Great Britain. If on
> the one hand there is no important industry
> employing a large number of highly skilled and
> highly paid workers, on the other hand there are
> no large industries (though unfortunately there are
> isolated small businesses) where wages are excep-
> tionally low."

We turn now to the information we have gathered
about the standard of living of the working-class
people in York.

Exact information, taken from their wage books, has
been furnished by employers regarding the average
weekly earnings of the householders in the families
visited by our investigators. If the wife went out to
work as well as the husband, information about her
average earnings was also given. In most cases the
figures given were the average earnings for a period of
three months, but some were for shorter and some for

longer periods. In the case of employers who only had one or two people working for them, such as a shop-keeper with one or two assistants, a highly qualified investigator called on the employer and obtained the information required.

We sought information about average *earnings* rather than about *wages*, because it took into account over-time, short time and piece-work earnings.

Altogether we have succeeded in obtaining information from the employers' wage books for over 95% of the heads of the households we called on. Where a man and wife were both working we obtained information about both their earnings. In the few cases where the employer refused to give information, we ascertained the current earnings in the industries concerned. As it may be thought that we were asking for information which should not properly have been divulged, we give below a copy of the letter sent by B. S. Rowntree to employers asking for information about the earnings of their employees:

Dear ————,

In 1900 I made a very detailed social survey in York with a view to ascertaining the conditions under which the working people were living. I made a second survey in 1936, which showed that the standard of life of the workers was 30% higher than in 1900. I am now engaged in making a third survey, with a view to ascertaining how far the welfare measures (e.g., family allowances, increased pensions, unemployment benefit, etc.) have succeeded in abolishing poverty.

In 1936 my investigators visited every working-class house in the city. This time they are only visiting one in ten.

In order that I may correctly assess the economic state of the workers, it is, of course, necessary that I should know what are their average net earnings (that is earnings after Income Tax and National Insurance have been deducted). It is in connection with this matter that I am obliged to seek the help of the employers in York, and the purpose of this letter is to appeal to you for your assistance.

I see that ——— of those on whom my investigators called are employed by you, and I should be immensely grateful if you would insert information about their net earnings on the attached sheet opposite the names of the persons indicated. I can assure you that if you are willing to do so, the information will be treated as strictly confidential and will be seen by nobody except myself and my secretaries. The investigators will not see it. In fact, the enquiry is as impersonal as a national census.

I think I should add that the information I seek is being given by all the large industrial concerns, by Government departments and by nationalised industries, with the approval of the Trade Unions. I am conscious, therefore, that although I am trespassing on your time, my request is not otherwise one that you need hesitate to grant.

Yours faithfully,

B. S. ROWNTREE.

Having obtained information about the earnings of the families visited by our investigators, the next step was to ascertain as accurately as possible what is the minimum sum required by families of different sizes to provide the necessities of healthy living. This information is given in the following chapter.

CHAPTER TWO

DETERMINATION OF THE POVERTY LINE

Expenditure on food

We have adopted the same dietary as in 1936 except for small modifications which it was necessary to make and which do not materially affect the total nutritive value of the dietary. For instance, we have substituted white flour for wholemeal flour, since the former is heavily subsidised and the latter is not. It takes about 23½ lb. of white flour to provide the calories contained in 16½ lb. of wholemeal flour, and we include this amount in our dietary. We have also assumed that bread is bought from the baker instead of being baked at home, since this is not practicable in many modern stoves. As fresh milk is heavily subsidised and condensed milk is not, we have substituted 14 pints of fresh milk for 12 tins of skimmed condensed milk equivalent to 14 pints of skimmed milk. We have added 18 oz. of sugar to the dietary, partly to replace that contained in the condensed skimmed milk, and also to bring the total amount of sugar up to the full ration.* We have cut down the cheese from 1 lb. to 10 oz. since the 1 lb. allowed in the 1936 dietary is in excess of the present ration. For the same reason we have cut the bacon from 1½ lb. to 1¼ lb. and the ration of cooking fat from 20 oz. to 10 oz. To make up for these we have added 1 lb. margarine.

School children receive one-third of a pint of milk a day during about 180 days a year, equal to one-sixth

* The ration of sugar includes the special allowances, which have been roughly averaged over the whole year.

of a pint throughout the year.* If we take this into account, the following table reflects the effect of the changes between the 1936 and 1950 dietaries:

	Calories	Protein (grammes)
Deduct from 1936 *diet*:		
Replacement of skimmed condensed milk by fresh full cream milk	3,010	28.0
Cheese, 6 oz.	702	42.6
Bacon (streaky), 4 oz. ..	516	8.8
Dripping and suet, 10 oz. ..	2,530	—
	6,758	79.4
Add to 1936 *diet*:		
School milk for three children, 3½ pints	1,190	63.0
Margarine, 16 oz.	3,488	—
Sugar, 18 oz.	1,944	—
	6,622	63.0

As the total number of calories in the dietary is nearly 80,000 and the amount of protein over 2,400 grammes, it will be seen that the effect of the modifications of the diet which have been made are quite insignificant. This dietary provides, for a family with three children under fourteen, the number of calories and the amount of protein which were regarded as adequate by a Committee of the British Medical Association set up in 1933. The nutritional requirements of the husband have been calculated on the assumption that he is engaged in work of moderate severity. It also provides the calories and protein for

* Probably the mother buys more milk than the 14 pints referred to above when the children get none at school, and less when they do get it.

women and children according to the standards laid down by that Committee.*

In 1947 the Council of the British Medical Association set up a Commission to examine the whole question of nutrition in this country. Twenty-seven experts served on it, and their report was published in 1950.

"Nutrition", they say, "is a young and rapidly growing science. Much of the field is still unexplored or is only half explored . . . and yet to-day's knowledge should be on record because it is the best we have by which to implement the basic facts of nutrition in terms of clinical medicine and public hygiene."

The Committee draw attention to "The need for more detailed information concerning the wide range of energy requirements within groups of the population, divided according to sex, age or occupation", and state that "Until data suitable for statistical treatment are available the choice of a calorie allowance for any one group must be to a large extent an uncertain one."

They add, however, that "To say this is not to cast serious doubt on the value of the calorie estimates that have been widely used in recent years in calculating the amount of food needed to nourish large groups of people, but is intended to emphasise the fact that such estimates lack precision. On the other hand, the wide and varied experience of problems of nutrition gained

* We are much indebted to Miss Schulz of the Oxford University Institute of Statistics who calculated the calories, protein, mineral salts, and vitamins in the dietary as amended. The detailed statement prepared by Miss Schulz showing the nutritive value of each item of food in the dietary will be found in the Appendix, pages 96 and 97.

The dietary adopted in 1936 was based on calculations made by Mr. Stanley Tennant. B. S. Rowntree told him of the work that we were doing and of the slight modifications which we were obliged to make in the 1936 dietary. On his own initiative Mr. Tennant calculated the calories and protein (but not the mineral salts and vitamins) in the amended dietary and got results almost exactly identical with those of Miss Schulz.

since 1939 provides convincing evidence that these calorie estimates were certainly of the right order of magnitude."

Study of the report has convinced us that the amount of calories and protein provided in the dietary accords with the best knowledge at present available, and the dietary is not deficient in iron or vitamins, and also provides a fair amount of calcium.*

The following is the dietary adopted:

DIETARY

	s.	d.
Breast of mutton—2½ lb. at 8d. per lb. (imported)	1	8
Minced beef—2 lb. at 1s. 4d. per lb. ..	2	8
Shin of beef—1½ lb. at 1s. 6d. per lb. ..	2	3
Liver—1 lb. at 1s. 6d. per lb.	1	6
Beef sausages—1 lb. at 1s. 3d. per lb. ..	1	3
Bacon—1¼ lb. at 1s. 11d. per lb. (cheapest cut)	2	4¾
Cheese—10 oz. at 1s. 2d. per lb. ..		8¾
Fresh full cream milk—14 pints at 5d. per pint	5	10
Herrings—1½ lb. at 8d. per lb.	1	0
Kippers—1 lb. at 1s. per lb. ..	1	0
Sugar—3 lb. 2 oz. at 5d. per lb. ..	1	3½
Potatoes—14 lb. at 9 lb. for 1s. ..	1	6½
23½ lb. bread—13½ loaves at 5½d. each ..	6	2¼
Oatmeal—2 lb. at 6d. per lb.	1	0
Margarine—2½ lb. at 10d. per lb.	2	1
Cooking fat—10 oz. at 1s. per lb.		7½
Flour—1¼ lb. at 9½d. per 3 lb. bag		4
Jam—1 lb. at 1s. 2d. per lb.	1	2
Treacle—1 lb. at 10d. (in tins)		10
Cocoa—¼ lb. at 8½d. per ¼ lb.		8½
Rice—10 oz. at 9d. per lb.		5½
Sago—¼ lb. at 9d. per lb.		2¼
Barley—2 oz. at 9d. per lb.		1
Peas—½ lb. at 10½d. per lb.		5¼

* There is no general agreement as to the amount of calcium required.

	s.	d.
Lentils—¾ lb. at 10½d. per lb.		8
Stoned dates—½ lb. at 10½d. per lb.		5¼
Swedes—6 lb. at 2½d. per lb.	1	3
Onions—4½ lb. at 5d. per lb.	1	10½
Apples—4 lb. at 5d. per lb.	1	8
Egg—1 at 3½d.		3½
Extra vegetables and fruit	1	6
Tea—½ lb. at 3s. 4d. per lb.	1	8
Extras, including salt, seasoning, etc.*		9
	47	4†

This dietary is for a man, wife, and three children under fourteen.

A woman requires 83% as much food as a man, and the requirements of children vary according to sex and age.‡ The dietary has a "man value" of 3.78. In calculating the necessary expenditure for food we allow 12s. 6½d. for a man, 10s. 5d. for a woman, and 8s. 1½d. for each child.

Expenditure on clothing for women and children and for household sundries

A woman investigator interviewed twenty-nine women in order to ascertain how much they spent on clothing for themselves and their children, and on household sundries. All of them were women whose husbands earned less than £6 a week. In the following table the annual expenditure under the different headings is given for the twenty-nine women. It will be noted that varying degrees of economy are practised in women's clothing, children's clothing, and household sundries respectively.

* Some seasoning, e.g., two Oxo cubes, will make rather dull dishes more palatable.

† This dietary was drawn up in the early part of October, 1950. The prices of the different items are based on information gathered by an investigator who visited a number of shops which cater for working-class people.

‡ The relation between the food requirements of men, women, and children are based on tables prepared by Cathcart and Murray, which are now generally accepted.

| Women's clothing and repairs | Children's clothing and repairs | | Household sundries |
	Total Expenditure	Expenditure per child	
£ s. d.	£ s. d.	£ s. d.	£ s. d.
50 14 2	50 16 0	25 8 0	39 7 11
46 17 7	32 17 8	16 8 10	26 0 9
46 6 5	34 11 11	34 11 11	20 9 4½
44 6 4½	13 14 2	13 14 2	17 15 9
43 8 1	72 9 3	24 3 1	29 18 2½
41 6 9	50 14 9	50 14 9	26 6 6
35 1 11	35 8 8	35 8 8	21 11 6½
34 18 0	61 10 5½	30 15 3	20 1 2½
33 5 1½	51 2 6	17 0 10	20 10 8½
31 8 4	22 0 4	22 0 4	23 7 8
30 11 4	32 19 1	32 19 1	20 12 11
30 6 7	43 8 8	14 9 7	20 12 3½
29 18 9	29 5 2	29 5 2	25 14 2
28 10 10	25 14 0	25 14 0	20 12 3
28 4 7	75 3 11	25 1 4	30 8 9
28 4 1	14 16 7	14 16 7	15 18 8
27 15 9	120 9 3	30 2 4	24 8 6
26 18 4½	53 18 0	53 18 0	21 2 0½
25 10 4	52 10 9	17 10 3	18 6 5
25 9 2	27 13 10	27 13 10	17 11 10
23 9 0	34 19 0	17 9 6	18 2 6
23 7 10	49 15 6½	16 11 10	18 4 8
22 10 3	38 12 0	19 6 0	16 16 0½
22 3 9½	58 1 9	19 7 3	20 6 10
18 16 0	61 0 0	30 10 0	23 14 2½
15 15 0½	47 0 3	15 13 5	18 12 9
15 0 11½	35 3 4	17 11 8	22 9 0½
14 2 4	54 4 2	18 1 5	14 4 0
11 4 1	134 4 9	22 7 5½	30 16 0½

The column showing the expenditure on clothing is arranged in order from the highest to the lowest. The columns showing the expenditure on children's clothing and household sundries are so arranged that each entry represents the expenditure of the woman whose expenditure on her own clothing is shown on the same line in the first column.

The average expenditure on women's clothing and repairs was 11s. 4d. a week, which included 5½d. for boot repairs, and on children's clothing and repairs was 9s. 6d. per week. In view of the great variation in the expenditure on women's, children's, and men's clothing, it would be misleading if we were to base our poverty line on the *average* expenditure incurred by all the families who supplied us with information. As we were anxious to establish a poverty line which no one could reasonably claim is too high, we based it on the average expenditure of the three women whose expenditure on clothing was the lowest, and have done the same in the case of expenditure on children's clothing and household sundries. The figures are 5s. 2d. a week for women's clothing, 5s. 6d. for children's clothing, and 6s. for household sundries.

Expenditure on men's clothing and for fuel and light

Interviews similar to those held with twenty-nine women were held with thirty-two men, and their annual expenditure on clothing and repairs was ascertained. The investigator also obtained information about their expenditure on coal, coke, electricity and gas in the summer and winter months respectively. The annual expenditure on clothing and on fuel are shown in the following table.

Men's clothing and repairs			Fuel and light			Men's clothing and repairs			Fuel and light		
£	s.	d.	£	s.	d.	£	s.	d.	£	s.	d.
44	0	0	34	18	0	24	15	7	31	4	0
40	0	7	30	15	8	24	14	8	17	10	0
34	15	6	34	6	0	23	15	0	28	17	0
33	7	3	22	10	0	22	10	2	33	14	0
32	15	0	30	4	0	22	3	0	31	12	0
32	3	11	35	3	0	21	3	9	32	6	0
31	19	2	19	9	0	20	4	2	34	2	0
31	18	8	29	0	0	19	13	7	32	18	0
31	4	10	32	0	0	18	14	1½	27	17	0
30	8	9	26	1	0	18	12	10½	31	6	0
30	3	6	26	10	0	18	11	8	38	4	8
29	10	8	25	8	0	18	5	0	31	4	0
28	3	6	35	14	0	17	4	7	27	16	0
26	17	2	37	15	6	16	18	2	32	1	0
25	16	2	31	10	0	16	7	0	32	8	0
24	18	5	30	6	0	14	3	7	25	10	0

The columns showing the expenditure on clothing are arranged in order from the highest to the lowest. Those showing the expenditure on fuel and light are so arranged that each entry represents the expenditure of the man whose expenditure on clothing is shown on the same line in the first column.

The average expenditure of all the men was 9s. 11d. on clothing and repairs, which included 6½d. for boot repairs, and 11s. 8d. on fuel and light, but, as in the case of the women, for the purpose of building up our poverty line we have taken the average expenditure of the three men whose expenditure was the lowest. This was 6s. 1d. a week for clothing and 7s. 7d. for fuel and light.

In 1936 B. S. Rowntree obtained information about expenditure on clothing in the same way as we have done. With regard to men's clothing, he wrote, "If we rule out certain estimates which were very much higher than the rest, of the twelve remaining replies the estimates vary from 2s. 6d. to 3s. 6d. and we shall not be far out if we adopt a figure of 3s. In the case of women's clothing, twelve estimates varied from 1s. 6½d. to 2s. 4½d. and I take 1s. 9d. as my figure".* He obtained forty estimates of the cost of necessary clothing for children of different ages, about which he wrote, "They point pretty generally to the conclusion that in making an all-round estimate of 1s. 1d. per week for children we should not be far from the truth."

None of these estimates included the cost of repairs. These are especially heavy to-day in the case of children's clothing. The materials of which they are made, especially boots, do not wear so well as those used in 1936. Taking the twenty-nine families whose expenditure was investigated in 1950, the cost of repairing children's boots and shoes averaged 9½d. per child per week.

In 1950 the variations in expenditure were very much greater than in 1936. In the case of women's clothing they varied from 4s. 4d. a week to 19s. 6d., in children's clothing from 5s. 3d. to 20s. 9d., and in men's clothing from 5s. 5d. to 16s. 11d. a week. The reason why the variations in the expenditure per head were so much

* "The Human Needs of Labour", pp. 94 and 95.

greater in 1950 than in 1936 is doubtless because working-class families are enjoying increased prosperity, and so there is a marginal sum of money available, after paying for the bare necessities of life, which can be spent according to personal inclination.

Household sundries

In computing the poverty line the amount allowed for household sundries for a man, wife, and three children is 6s. The question arises of how to divide it for families of different composition.

Some items of expenditure will not be affected to any significant extent by the size of the family (e.g., dustpans, pails, sweeping brushes), others will vary to a certain extent (e.g., sheets, towels, crockery, and household soap), and the expenditure on other items will vary strictly in accordance with the number of members in the family (e.g., toothbrushes, toilet soap, etc.).

Clearly it is impossible to get a mathematically accurate figure showing the amount to allow for families of different sizes. After a careful study of the facts available we have decided to allow the following sums for families of various sizes:

Number of persons	Amount allowed for household sundries per week
	s. d.
1	2 5
2	3 10
3	5 0
4	5 8
5	6 0
6	6 4
7	6 8

This is an estimate only. In the case of food, clothing, and fuel and light we can give precise figures, but the total amount involved for household sundries is only 6s., which is a small proportion of the total expenditure, and therefore any inaccuracy there may be in the division of household sundries for families of different sizes is unimportant.

Examples of expenditure on clothes and household sundries

On the following pages we give typical schedules referring to clothing and repairs and to household sundries which show the character of the information which we obtained. They refer in each case to one of the three families on whose expenditure our poverty line is based, i.e., one of the three families whose expenditure was the lowest.

Women's clothing and repairs

Approximate age 38, married, with three children of school age. Annual expenditure on clothing and repairs was £14 2s. 4d.

Clothing bought	How often	Cost			Cost per annum		
		£	s.	d.	£	s.	d.
Dress	One in three years	2	2	0		14	0
Coat and skirt	One a year (second-hand)		12	6		12	6
Odd skirt	One a year (second-hand)		2	6		2	6
Overcoat	One in three years	6	6	0	2	2	0
Raincoat or mackintosh	One a year (second-hand)		12	6		12	6
Blouse	None		—			—	
Jumper (ready made)	One a year (second-hand)		3	6		3	6
Cardigan (ready made)	None		—			—	
Wool to knit jumper or cardigan	None						
Hat	One in three years		17	6		5	10
Head-scarf	None		—			—	
Shoes	One pair in two years	1	10	0		15	0
Slippers	None		—			—	
Stockings	Twelve pairs a year	1	16	0	1	16	0
Under-slip	One a year		7	6		7	6
Vest	Two a year		11	0		11	0
Knickers	Four pairs a year	1	6	0	1	6	0
Corsets	One pair a year	1	1	0	1	1	0
Brassiere	None		—			—	
Nightdress (or pyjamas)	Two in two years	1	10	0		15	0
Apron	Three a year		12	0		12	0
Gloves (ready made)	None		—			—	
Wool to knit gloves	One pair a year		2	0		2	0
Handkerchiefs	Two a year		2	0		2	0
					12	0	4
Shoes repaired once in three months at 10s. 6d. a time					2	2	0
Repairs and dry cleaning of clothes						Nil	
					£14	2	4

Children's clothing and repairs

Family with three children; one girl aged 10 months, one girl aged 2 years and one boy aged 5½ years. Annual expenditure on clothing and repairs £43 8s. 8d., i.e., £14 9s. 7d. for each child.

Clothing bought	How often	Cost	Cost per annum
		£ s. d.	£ s. d.
Terry squares .. ⎫ Nappies.. .. ⎭	Bought this year ..	1 11 8	1 11 8
Baby's gown	None	—	—
Baby's dress (day) ..	Four a year	2 16 0	2 16 0
Baby's dress (night) ..	Three a year	18 6	18 6
Baby's woollies (outdoor and indoor)	Two a year (knits her own)	15 0	15 0
Boots (or shoes) ..	Nine pairs every year ..	5 8 6	5 8 6
Socks (or stockings) ..	Nineteen pairs every year	1 6 10	1 6 10
Overcoat	Three every year ..	8 0 0	8 0 0
Raincoat or mackintosh	One every year ..	1 10 0	1 10 0
Blouse (girl's)	None	—	—
Shirt (boy's)	Six every year	2 5 0	2 5 0
Handkerchiefs	Six every year	4 6	4 6
Pullover (or jersey or jumper)	Five every year.. ..	3 3 0	3 3 0
Vest	Six every year	14 0	14 0
Knickers (girl's) ..	Six pairs every year ..	17 6	17 6
Under pants (boy's) ..	Two pairs every year ..	7 10	7 10
Suit (boy's)	None	—	—
Odd trousers (boy's) ..	Four pairs every year ..	2 11 8	2 11 8
Dress (girl's)	Two every year ..	1 8 0	1 8 0
Odd skirt (girl's) ..	One every year ..	1 7 11	1 7 11
Collars (boy's)	None	—	—
Tie (boy's)	None	—	—
Cap, hat or head-scarf..	One every year ..	3 6	3 6
Nightdress (or pyjamas)	Four pairs every year ..	1 15 3	1 15 3
Gloves	Two pairs every year ..	10 10	10 10
Braces or belt (boy's) ..	Two pairs every year ..	7 10	7 10
			38 3 4
Shoes repaired every three weeks at 5s. 6d. a time ..		..	4 15 4
Repairs and dry cleaning of clothes		..	10 0
			£43 8 8

Mens' clothing and repairs

Approximate age 32, married, with one child. Annual expenditure on clothing and repairs £14 3s. 7d.

Clothing bought	How often	Cost			Cost per annum		
		£	s.	d.	£	s.	d.
Suit	One every five years	7	10	0	1	10	0
Overcoat	Not worn		—			—	
Raincoat	One every three years	4	10	0	1	10	0
Odd trousers	One every three years	2	19	0		19	8
Sports jacket	One every three years	5	0	0	1	13	4
Pullover	One every five years (knitted by wife)		14	0		2	10
Shoes	One pair every eighteen months	2	0	0	1	6	8
Hat	One every five years	1	3	0		4	7
Shirt	One every year	1	5	0	1	5	0
Collars	Two every year		3	0		3	0
Under vests	One every year		4	1		4	1
Under pants	One pair every year		3	11		3	11
Socks	Four pairs every year		12	0		12	0
Handkerchiefs	Four every year		5	0		5	0
Necktie	One every year		8	6		8	6
Scarf	Not worn		—			—	
Pyjamas (or nightshirt)	One every year	1	0	0	1	0	0
Overall	One every year	1	5	0	1	5	0
Braces	One pair every year		5	0		5	0
Three pairs of shoes repaired a year (two repaired at home by himself. One sent to shop for repair)					12	18	7
					1	0	0
One suit cleaned						5	0
					£14	3	7

Household sundries

Family consists of man, wife, and three children. Annual expenditure on household sundries £14 4s. 0d.

Articles bought	How often	Cost			Cost per annum		
		£	s.	d.	£	s.	d.
Towels	Six a year	1	15	0	1	15	0
Tea towels	Odd pieces	—			—		
Tablecloths	One a year (plastic) ..	1	5	0	1	5	0
Blankets	Very rarely*	—			—		
Sheets	One pair a year ..	1	10	0	1	10	0
Pillow-cases	Four a year		16	0		16	0
Dusters	None	—			—		
Curtains	Very rarely	—			—		
Saucepans	One a year		6	9		6	9
Other cooking utensils..	About once a year ..		7	6		7	6
Pails	One in two years ..		5	0		2	6
Crockery	Odd cups yearly ..		10	0		10	0
Sweeping brush ..	One in five years ..		7	6		1	6
Scrubbing brush ..	One a year		2	6		2	6
Boot brushes	One set in seven years		5	6			9
Broom	None	—			—		
Dustpan	One a year		3	6		3	6
Toothbrushes (for all the family)	Five a year		7	6		1	6
Shopping bag or basket	None	—			—		
					7	2	6
Household soap ..					1	10	0
Toilet soap						18	0
Cleansing powders (all kinds)					2	5	0
Toothpaste						18	0
Soda						6	6
Floor polish					—		
Boot polish					1	4	0
					£14	4	0

* See p. 25, where it is stated that 10s. is allowed to young married couples.

Personal sundries

Up to this point our estimates about the necessary expenditure on food, clothing, household sundries, fuel, and lighting are based on carefully ascertained facts, but in the matter of expenditure on personal sundries we are obliged very largely to rely on our own judgment in deciding what items to include. We must bear in mind that our object is to arrive at a reliable estimate of the proportion of the working-class population of York who are living in primary poverty, i.e., poverty due to lack of income, no matter how carefully the income is spent.

In the 1936 survey 9s. was allowed for personal sundries for a family of five persons, and in order to enable the readers to judge whether that allowance was liberal or otherwise, the following table was given showing what it would buy:

	s.	d.
Unemployment and Health Insurance ..	1	7
Contribution to sick and burial clubs ..	1	0
Trade Union subscription		6
Travelling to and from work..	1	0
Such necessaries as stamps, writing-paper, etc., for the family		6
A daily newspaper		7
Wireless		6
All else: beer, tobacco, presents, holidays, books, travelling, etc.	3	4
	9	0

As the payment for Unemployment and Health Insurance are now compulsory, they (and any Income Tax payable) have been deducted from wages in the figures showing the workers' earnings, and therefore they do not appear under the heading of personal sundries. Although the statutory benefits under the

Health Scheme are more liberal than they were, payment to a sick club is still necessary, for, of course, the statutory benefit falls much below the normal earnings of men and women at work. Contributions to a burial club are also usual, notwithstanding the death grant of £20 for an adult, and grants varying from £5 to £15 according to age for children under 18. A funeral is to-day a very expensive affair. Working people make great sacrifices to ensure their dead are buried with due respect. We therefore include 1s. for expenditure on sick and burial clubs in our estimate of personal sundries. In the case of men, we have raised the figure for the expenditure on Trade Union subscriptions from 6d. to 9d. We have not altered the cost of travelling to and from work, but have doubled the sum allowed for stamps, writing-paper, etc., in view of the increase in the postage rates, which took place in 1940, and the increase in the cost of other items coming under this heading, and we have added 1d. to the cost of a daily newspaper as Sunday newspapers now cost 2d. We have also doubled the amount allowed for "All else". Even this sum will not buy anything like as much as 3s. 4d. did in 1936. These modifications raise the sum allowed for personal sundries for a family of five from 9s. to 11s. 6d., assuming that the man is in employment.

	s.	d.
Contribution to sick and burial clubs ..	1	0
Trade Union subscription (man)		9
Travelling to and from work..	1	0
Stamps, writing-paper, etc.	1	0
Daily newspaper		8
Wireless		*5
All else: beer, tobacco, presents, holidays, books, travelling, etc.	6	8
	11	6

* This is 1d. less than the figure given in 1936 because now comparatively few people have to buy batteries. The small cost of electricity for a wireless set is included in the expenditure on fuel and light.

If the man and wife are *both* working the figure allowed for personal sundries has been increased by 1s. 6d.— 1s. for travelling to and from work for the woman, and 6d. for her Trade Union subscription. If the chief wage-earner is a woman, the allowance of 6s. 8d. for "All else" would be reduced to 5s. and the Trade Union subscription from 9d. to 6d. In the case of unemployed persons we have deducted the Trade Union subscription, because on the schedules almost all of those who are unemployed are sick and have been unemployed for a very long time. We have also deducted the 1s. for travelling to and from work.

Adding together the necessary weekly expenditure, excluding rent, under different headings for a family of five, we arrive at a total of £5 0s. 2d., made up as follows:

Food

	£	s.	d.	£	s.	d.
Man		12	6½			
Woman		10	5			
Three children	1	4	4½			
				2	7	4

Clothing

	£	s.	d.	£	s.	d.
Man		6	1			
Woman		5	2			
Three children		16	6			
				1	7	9
Household sundries ..					6	0
Fuel and light					7	7
Personal sundries					11	6
				£5	0	2

In 1936 B. S. Rowntree made an allowance of 5s. a week for a young married couple with one child, and 3s. for a couple with two children. In connection with these allowances he wrote:

> "This item for saving has been included in the necessary expenditure in the case of young married couples, for it is a rare occurrence for a young couple to start their married life with a house so fully furnished as to meet even the minimum requirements of a family. My cost of living standard only allows for the maintenance of a fully furnished house. It allows nothing for the purchase of furniture and bedding, or for other similar expenditure of a non-recurring nature."*

In view of the increased cost of living we have allowed 10s. for a young couple with one child, and 6s. if there are two children. It was necessary to fix arbitrarily the age at which married couples cease to be "young" for the purpose of this allowance, and we decided that it should be the thirtieth birthday of the chief wage earner.

* "Poverty and Progress", p. 31.

CHAPTER THREE

THE NUMBER OF PEOPLE IN POVERTY

We have explained in Chapter 1 how we obtained information about the earnings of the householder and of his wife (if she went out to work). In assessing the available income of each family there are, however, other items to be taken into account.

Our investigators ascertained in almost all cases how much children in employment and lodgers paid to the householder for board and lodging. In the few cases where this information was not forthcoming we assumed that they paid the average amount.

Of sources of income other than wages, the following are the most important:

Retirement Pensions, formerly called Old Age Pensions.

Widows' Pensions.

Industrial Pensions.

War Pensions.

Family allowances. (5s. per child after the first).

Grants by the Assistance Board as supplementary pensions for the aged, and in other cases of need.

Payments from the National Insurance Fund in cases of unemployment or sickness.

Most of these various types of payments are fixed by statute and there was thus no difficulty in arriving at the actual sums received by the families concerned. In the case of industrial pensions we adopted the same procedure as with wages and, with suitable safeguards to ensure that there was no breach of confidence, we obtained details of actual individual pensions from the pensioners' former employers.

In arriving at the total available income it was necessary, in addition to the foregoing, to include various miscellaneous sources of income, namely:

The net value of vegetables grown in allotments or gardens. This, after discussion with a number of working-class men and women, we assessed at 7s. 6d. a week where all vegetables were home grown, and 5s. and 2s. 6d. where "most" and "some" respectively were grown.

The value of free milk at school and of free meals in the very few cases where, because of family circumstances, the latter are given without the normal charge. On the basis of one-third of a pint of milk per day for five days in each week of the school year, we have estimated the value of free milk at 9d. per child per week of the calendar year. As school meals normally cost 2s. 6d. per week we have allowed a sum of 1s. 11d. per week when meals are free, the difference being again because of the difference between the school and calendar years.

The value of cheap milk allowed to infants below school age. At the rate of 1½d. per pint per child each day instead of 5d., we have allowed 1s. 9d. per child per week for the first two children, with a sharp reduction thereafter to keep the total assumed purchases of milk within the limits allowed in our dietary.

Taking all the foregoing sources of income into account we were able to ascertain with a high degree of accuracy what was the total available income of each family.

To deduce from that information how many families were in poverty, it was necessary first to deduct from the total income of each family payments made by that family in respect of rent and rates (exact information about which was obtained by our investigators), and then to relate the residual income to the poverty line for the family concerned.

In Chapter 2 we explained how the poverty line was determined, and we showed that a family consisting of a man, wife, and three children required an income of £5 0s. 2d., after paying rent and rates, if they were to be above the poverty line. The following table shows the amount required for differently constituted families:

	Employed			Unemployed		
	£	s.	d.	£	s.	d.
Man alone	1	16	1	1	17	11
Woman alone	1	11	1	1	13	2
Two women living together ..	2	14	7	2	14	1
Man and woman	2	17	2	2	16	2
Man, woman, and one child ..	3	11	11	3	10	11
Man, woman, and two children	4	6	4	4	5	4
Man, woman, and three children	5	0	2	4	19	2

Add 14s. for each additional dependent child.

Add 15s. 11d. for each additional dependent adult female.

Add 19s. for each additional dependent adult male.

Add 10s. 9d.* for each adult female lodger.

Add 12s. 11d.* for each adult male lodger.

Add 23s. 8d.* for adult male and female lodgers.

Add 8s. 3d.* for each child lodger.

Working on the above basis we have divided the families into the following classes according to their available income after paying rent and rates:

Class

'A'	Under 77s.†	
'B'	77s. and under 100s.	For man, wife, and three children, or the equiv-alent of that income in the case of differently constituted families.
'C'	100s. and under 123s.	
'D'	123s. and under 146s.	
'E'	146s. and over	

From the foregoing it will be seen that a family with an available income of 100s. would be placed in Class 'C' if it consisted of a man, wife, and two children, in Class 'E' if there were no children, in Class 'B' if there were four children, and in Class 'A' if there were five children.

In summarising the results of his investigations in 1936, B. S. Rowntree drew up the following table:

---

* Food and increment of household sundries only.

† 77s. is the equivalent of 33s. 6d. in 1936 and 23s. the equivalent of 10s.

For the purpose of this table we have taken the income required to enable a family of man, wife, and three children to live above the poverty line as being £5 per week, after paying rent, instead of £5 0s. 2d. The incomes include the grants to young married couples referred to on p. 25.

Class			No. of persons	Percentage of working-class population (excluding domestic servants and persons in public institutions)	Percentage of total population
'A'	Under 33s. 6d.	Available income for man, wife, and three children, or its equivalent for differently constituted families	7,837	14.2	8.1
'B'	33s. 6d. to 43s. 5d.		9,348	16.9	9.6
'C'	43s. 6d. to 53s. 5d.		10,433	18.9	10.8
'D'	53s. 6d. to 63s. 5d.		7,684	13.9	8.0
'E'	63s. 6d. and over		19,904	36.1	20.5
'F'	Domestic Servants.. ..		4,300	—	4.4
'G'	Working class in institutions		3,530	—	3.6
'H'	Remainder of population (including Acomb)		33,944	—	35.0
			96,980	100.0	100.0

In 1936 there were 4,300 domestic servants. These would not be in poverty. The number will be much smaller now, probably not more than 1,000.

In 1936 3,530 working-class people were in institutions of various kinds. A considerable proportion of them were in the Public Assistance Institution, formerly called the workhouse. Others were in hospitals or mental hospitals. As all of these were receiving board and lodging they could not be included among those living in poverty. We have no exact information of the number of persons receiving institutional care in 1950, for the changes brought about by the National Health Service Act, and the National Assistance Act (including the abolition of the Poor Law, and therefore of the Public Assistance Institutions), makes it more difficult to compute them. In any case, since this book deals only with economic matters, the exact number is immaterial, for persons in hospitals, mental hospitals and Homes will not be in poverty.

For purposes of comparison with the table drawn up by B. S. Rowntree and reproduced above, we have drawn up the following table, which gives the corresponding facts for 1950:

Class	Financial limits of the Class		No. of persons	Percentage of working-class population (excluding domestic servants and persons in public institutions)	Percentage of total population
'A'	Under 77s.	Available income for man, wife, and three children, or its equivalent for differently constituted families	234	0.37	0.23
'B'	77s. and under 100s.		1,512	2.40	1.43
'C'	100s. and under 123s.		12,096	19.23	11.48
'D'	123s. and under 146s.		12,429	19.76	11.90
'E'	146s. and over		36,585	58.24	34.98
'H'	Remainder of the population, including domestic servants and persons receiving care in hospitals or elsewhere under the National Health Service Act or the National Assistance Act		41,744	—	39.98
			104,600	100.00	100.00

The number of persons in each class in the two years 1936 and 1950 can be represented thus:

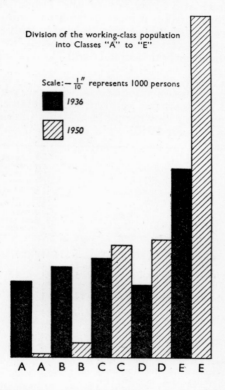

Division of the working-class population
into Classes "A" to "E"

Scale:— $\frac{1}{10}''$ represents 1000 persons

■ 1936

▨ 1950

A A   B B   C C   D D   E E

The foregoing diagram depicts the remarkable decrease in poverty between 1936 and 1950, even though the population of York has increased in that period by some 8,000 persons. A more exact diagrammatic comparison of the division of the working-class population into classes in each of the two years is given below. It shows the proportion of the working-class population in each class in each of the years.

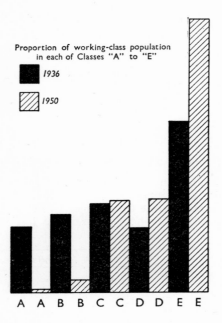

Proportion of working-class population
in each of Classes "A" to "E"

■ 1936

▨ 1950

A slightly different division of the working-class population into classes is obtained if it is made on the basis of families, instead of on the basis of individuals. In some respects a classification on the basis of families gives a more accurate picture of the situation because a family may be in poverty even though some member of it, such as a son or daughter in employment who is contributing only a part of his or her earnings to the family income, is not in poverty. In calculations on the basis of individuals such a person is inevitably, and wrongly, counted as in poverty.* Furthermore, statistics prepared on a family basis give due weight to the circumstances of persons, usually the aged, who are living alone, and who, as our investigations showed, constitute a large proportion of those who are in poverty. The division of the working-class population of York into Classes 'A' to 'E' on the family basis is given in the following table:

Class	No. of families	Percentage
'A'	81	0.41
'B'	765	4.23
'C'	3,510	19.40
'D'	3,141	17.38
'E'	10,602	58.58

An examination of the circumstances of the 846 families in York who are in poverty shows that the poverty is due to one or other of five causes. In the following table we show the relative importance of each:

Cause of poverty	Number of families			
	Class 'A'	Class 'B'	Classes 'A' and 'B' together	%
Sickness	36	144	180	21.3
Old age	36	540	576	68.1
Death of chief wage-earner	9	45	54	6.3
Large number of children	—	27	27	3.2
Low wages	—	9	9	1.1

Perhaps the most striking fact about the foregoing table is that not a single family is in poverty due to the unemployment of an able-bodied wage-earner,

* This was much less likely to be the case in 1936, as at that time the rules relating to the payment of benefits to the unemployed (then constituting 28.6% of all persons in poverty) included the "Means Test" which, in assessing benefit, took the earnings of sons and daughters into account. The "Means Test" has since been abolished.

although in a large proportion of the families classified as in poverty due to sickness the chief wage-earner is permanently unable to work because of his ailments.

Among the large percentage of cases where poverty is due to old age, a good many of the families concerned are in receipt of supplementary pensions, thus demonstrating that even with our stringent definition of poverty, supplementary pensions are no longer a guarantee against poverty. In this connection, however, we should point out that when old people are faced with some major expenditure they can, if necessary, obtain an "Exceptional Needs Grant" from the Assistance Board, so that they can normally concentrate their spending on immediate needs such as food and fuel. Consequently their situation may not be as bad as the foregoing analysis would otherwise suggest.

The following table, comparing the causes of poverty in 1936 and 1950, shows the changes that have occurred in the period between the two surveys.

Cause of poverty	Percentage of those in poverty	
	1936	1950
	%	%
Unemployment of chief wage-earner	28.6	Nil
Inadequate wages of earners in regular employment	32.8	1.0
Inadequate earnings of other workers	9.5	Nil
Old age	14.7	68.1
Death of chief wage-earner	7.8	6.4
Sickness	4.1	21.3
Miscellaneous	2.5	3.2

Our calculations, showing the actual amount of poverty in York in September, 1950, were completed before the Chancellor of the Exchequer announced in his budget speech in the House of Commons on the 10th April, 1951, that he proposed to increase the rates of retirement pensions from 26s. for a single person and 42s. for a man and his wife to 30s. and 50s. respectively.

It occurred to us that it would be useful to examine what effect these concessions would have had on the volume of poverty if they had been in force at the time of our investigation. We have accordingly made the necessary additional calculations and the results are set out in the following table:

EFFECT OF INCREASING THE RATES OF RETIREMENT PENSIONS

Class	Actual situation in 1950		Situation in 1950 if the increased rates of retirement pensions had been in force	
	Number of families	%	Number of families	%
'A'	81	0.41	54	0.30
'B'	765	4.23	297	1.65
'C'	3,510	19.40	3,600	19.89
'D'	3,141	17.38	3,348	18.49
'E'	10,602	58.58	10,800	59.67

These figures indicate how satisfactorily the increases in the retirement pensions deal with what was in 1950 by far the greatest remaining cause of poverty. But two facts must be remembered if we are tempted to conclude from the favourable figures that the problem of primary poverty has been finally overcome. First that, in the table showing the result of the increased pensions granted in the 1951 Budget, we have related a poverty line based on 1950 prices to increases of income granted in 1951 largely because of increased prices. This inevitably introduces some element of unreality into the calculations. Second, that the table necessarily reflects the situation at a time when, to all intents and purposes, there is no unemployment. We show in Chapter 5 what effect varying degrees of unemployment would have.

CHAPTER FOUR

TO WHAT EXTENT IS
THE REDUCTION IN POVERTY DUE TO
WELFARE LEGISLATION?

As we stated at the beginning of this book, our basic purpose in writing it was to demonstrate the extent to which poverty has been reduced by welfare measures introduced or extended since 1936. We have already shown in Chapter 3 how much poverty we found in 1950, and how the working-class population of the city was divided between the five economic classes, 'A' to 'E'. In this chapter we give the results of a series of calculations demonstrating first the effect of all the welfare measures together, and then the effect of each of the two most important ones.

Our first sets of calculations were aimed at ascertaining how the individuals and families would have been divided between Classes 'A' to 'E' if their gain from welfare legislation had been the same as in 1936. To arrive at the gain to each family we had to calculate the value of food subsidies, family allowances, school milk, cheap milk for infants, and free school meals where granted. To this figure we added the difference between retirement or widows' pensions in 1936 and 1950, and from the total we subtracted the difference between the individual's weekly contribution under the National Insurance Act and the corresponding contribution in 1936.

In deciding the figure to be allowed in our calculation for food subsidies we applied the figures given in the Ministry of Food Bulletin No. 585 of the 10th February 1951, to our poverty line diet. As a result we adopted the figure of 2s. 9d. as the value of the food subsidies to an adult male, 2s. 3d. to an adult female, and 1s. 6d. to each child.*

We were in some difficulty whether to take supplementary pensions into account when deciding on the total of the increased welfare benefits, since before the introduction of the supplementary pensions old people in need could obtain Public Assistance under the Poor Law. In fact, as is well known, a large proportion of old people preferred to put up with great privation rather than seek Public Assistance. Nevertheless, Public Assistance was obtainable and we have therefore disregarded supplementary pensions in calculating the net increase in welfare benefits. Had we taken the opposite course and included supplementary pensions the effect of the welfare measures in reducing poverty would have been somewhat greater than we show it to have been in the table given below. The difference would, however, not have been large, because, even with our stringent definition of poverty, an old person can, as we pointed out in Chapter 3, be in poverty even if he or she is in receipt of a supplementary pension.

The following table shows from our calculations how the working-class population of York would have been affected if in 1950 the welfare legislation had been the same as in 1936:

* These figures are lower than those given by the Minister of Food in a speech at Bradford on the 26th November, 1950, when he said, "The cash value of the food subsidies to people in this country is, on the average, 2s. 10d. for each person each week, and it is worth noting that our surveys show that everybody, whatever his income, does in fact benefit to that amount within a penny or two either way." We have preferred to take the lower figures based on calculations from the poverty line diet because we can then be sure that we are not exaggerating the effect of the food subsidies, and therefore the effect of the welfare measures as a whole.

EFFECT ON INDIVIDUALS OF ALL THE WELFARE MEASURES TAKEN TOGETHER

Class	1936	Actual situation in 1950		The situation in 1950 if welfare measures had been identical with those in force in 1936	
	%	No. of persons	%	No. of persons	%
'A'	14.2	234	0.37	2,970	4.72
'B'	16.9	1,512	2.40	10,971	17.46
'C'	18.9	12,096	19.23	9,378	14.93
'D'	13.9	12,429	19.76	10,692	17.01
'E'	36.1	36,585	58.24	28,845	45.88

Alternatively, the effect of the welfare measures can be expressed diagrammatically in the following form, where each pillar represents the size of the economic class whose letter stands below it. The solid black pillars represent the actual situation in 1950, and the shaded pillars show what the situation would have been if the welfare measures in 1950 had been identical with those in force in 1936:

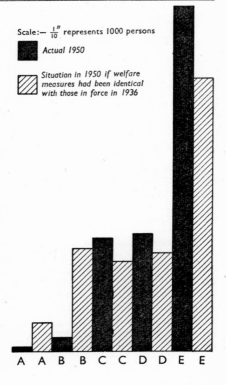

Scale:— $\frac{1}{10}''$ represents 1000 persons

Actual 1950

Situation in 1950 if welfare measures had been identical with those in force in 1936

A A B B C C D D E E

For the reasons explained in Chapter 3, a calculation on the basis of families instead of individuals gives slightly different results, and the following table shows how families would have been affected in 1950 if the welfare measures had been identical with those in force in 1936:

EFFECT ON FAMILIES OF ALL THE WELFARE MEASURES TAKEN TOGETHER

Class	Actual situation in 1950		The situation in 1950 if welfare measures had been identical with those in force in 1936	
	No. of families	%	No. of families	%
'A'	81	0.41	1,197	6.62
'B'	765	4.23	3,276	18.11
'C'	3,510	19.40	2,592	14.32
'D'	3,141	17.38	2,412	13.32
'E'	10,602	58.58	8,622	47.63

It will be seen from the table on page 39 that whereas the proportion of the working-class population living in poverty has been reduced since 1936 from 31.1% to 2.77% it would have been reduced to 22.18% if welfare legislation had remained unaltered.

Our next task was to make a further series of calculations to ascertain what would have been the effect on poverty in 1950 if there had been no food subsidies. The results of these calculations are set out below, and it will be seen that without food subsidies 13.74% of the individuals in the working class, comprising 16.59% of working-class families, would have been in poverty, as compared with actual figures, including food subsidies, of 2.77% of individuals comprising 4.64% of working-class families.

EFFECT ON INDIVIDUALS OF THE FOOD SUBSIDIES

Class	1936	Actual situation in 1950		The situation in 1950 if there had been no food subsidies	
	%	No. of persons	%	No. of persons	%
'A'	14.2	234	0.37	1,521	2.42
'B'	16.9	1,512	2.40	7,128	11.32
'C'	18.9	12,096	19.23	11,043	17.59
'D'	13.9	12,429	19.76	11,448	18.21
'E'	36.1	36,585	58.24	31,716	50.46

Alternatively, the effect of the food subsidies can be expressed diagrammatically in the following form, where each pillar represents the size of the economic class whose letter stands below it. The solid black pillars represent the actual situation in 1950, and the shaded pillars show what the situation would have been if there had been no food subsidies:

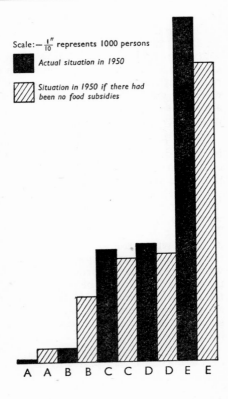

Scale:— $\frac{1}{10}''$ represents 1000 persons

Actual situation in 1950

Situation in 1950 if there had been no food subsidies

4

EFFECT ON FAMILIES OF THE FOOD SUBSIDIES

Class	Actual situation in 1950		The situation in 1950 if there had been no food subsidies	
	No. of families	%	No. of families	%
'A'	81	0.41	756	4.19
'B'	765	4.23	2,241	12.40
'C'	3,510	19.40	2,799	15.48
'D'	3,141	17.38	2,826	15.56
'E'	10,602	58.58	9,477	52.37

Our final calculations were to ascertain the effect of family allowances and the results are shown in the two following tables. They show that without family allowances the number of individuals in poverty would rise from 1,746 to 3,744, i.e., from 2.77% of the working class to 5.97%, and that without these allowances 6.46% of working-class families would be in poverty instead of 4.64%.

To be fully significant, however, the figures should be considered in relation to the number of families eligible to draw family allowances, i.e., those where there are two or more children. Our investigations showed that, among the working-class population of York, there are 2,655 families with one child, 1,196 with two, 396 with three, and 108 with four or more. The effect of the removal of family allowances would, as is shown in the table below, be to place 324 more families in poverty, equivalent to 19% of all families with two or more children. A further effect, not shown in the table, would be to place an additional 468 families in the lowest sub-division of Class 'C', where, as we point out in Chapter 9, conditions are so stringent that they are little better off than a family just in poverty.*

* The poverty line for a man, wife, and three children being £5 0s. 2d., the lowest sub-division of Class 'C' are those where the disposable income after paying rent and rates, is between £5 0s. 2d. and £5 5s. 10d. (or the equivalent of these amounts for differently constituted families).

EFFECT ON INDIVIDUALS OF FAMILY ALLOWANCES

Class	1936	Actual situation in 1950		The situation in 1950 if there had been no family allowances	
	%	No. of persons	%	No. of persons	%
'A'	14.2	234	0.37	486	0.79
'B'	16.9	1,512	2.40	3,258	5.18
'C'	18.9	12,096	19.23	12,276	19.53
'D'	13.9	12,429	19.76	12,159	19.35
'E'	36.1	36,585	58.24	34,677	55.15

Alternatively, the effect of family allowances can be expressed diagrammatically in the following form, where each pillar represents the size of the economic class whose letter stands below it. The solid black pillars represent the actual situation in 1950, and the shaded pillars show what the situation would have been if there had been no family allowances:

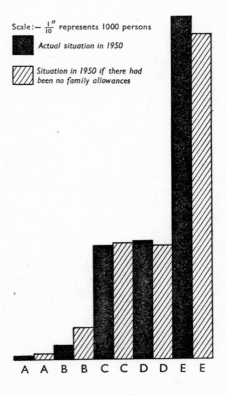

Scale:— $\frac{1}{10}''$ represents 1000 persons

Actual situation in 1950

Situation in 1950 if there had been no family allowances

A A   B B   C C   D D   E E

EFFECT ON FAMILIES OF FAMILY ALLOWANCES

Class	Actual situation in 1950		The situation in 1950 if there had been no family allowances	
	No. of families	%	No. of families	%
'A'	81	0.41	126	0.69
'B'	765	4.23	1,044	5.77
'C'	3,510	19.40	3,564	19.69
'D'	3,141	17.38	3,186	17.61
'E'	10,602	58.58	10,179	56.24

It will be noticed that in assessing the changes in welfare provisions since 1936 we have taken no account of three important matters, the National Health Service Act, the housing subsidies, and the extension of the principle of rent restriction.

As far as the National Health Service is concerned, it would have been impossible for us to make any worthwhile calculation of its economic effects, since a great many of its beneficiaries would previously have gone without spectacles and without medical and dental help. A proportion of them would, of course, in any case have paid for professional services. Their gain is not reflected in the tables on pages 39 and 40 showing the beneficial effect of welfare measures.

We deal, as far as we are able, with housing subsidies and rent restriction in Chapter 10. The economic gain to the working class from these subsidies is undoubtedly greater than in 1936 because a higher proportion of persons are living in council houses, all of which are subsidised, while rent restriction now applies to virtually every house in which working-class people live except council houses. Any accurate calculation of the economic benefit would be extremely difficult, and indeed almost impossible in the case of rent restriction. It should not, however, be entirely forgotten that besides the social benefits of good housing, the working class do obtain a considerable economic benefit, which is not reflected anywhere in our calculations in this chapter.

One final matter to which we wish to refer is the disappearance of unemployment as a cause of poverty. As stated in Chapter 3, no able-bodied person was found to be in poverty because of unemployment. The male householders who were unemployed despite being fit, and wishing to work, were all in Classes 'C' or 'D', since each of them had a source of income other than his unemployment insurance benefit. The rates of that benefit payable under the National Insurance Act are not alone sufficient to maintain a family above the poverty line even if the other welfare measures are taken into account. It follows that large-scale unemployment, such as occurred in the 1930s, could result in widespread poverty which would be alleviated, but not prevented, by the welfare legislation at present on the Statute Book. This question is examined further in the next chapter.

CHAPTER FIVE

WHAT WOULD BE THE EFFECT OF SERIOUS UNEMPLOYMENT?

As we pointed out at the end of Chapter 4, the reduction of unemployment to negligible proportions has been a factor of considerable importance in the reduction of poverty from its comparatively high level in 1936 to the low level we found in 1950.

We determined to examine how far a substantial amount of unemployment would affect the situation disclosed by our investigations.

Accordingly, we took all our schedules relating to families where the head of the household is in employment (i.e., rejecting those concerning pensioners, including widows, and the sick) and we placed them in a pile in no particular order. We then drew every twentieth schedule out of the pile.

On each of the schedules thus selected we disregarded the information about the earnings of the head of the household, and substituted a sum representing the unemployment benefit he would receive under the National Insurance Act if he were unemployed. We were thus able to calculate what proportion of the working-class families in York would be in each of our Classes 'A' to 'E' if 5% of the heads of households were unemployed. The result of our calculations is shown in the following table:

Class	Actual situation in 1950 (families)	Situation in 1950 with 5% unemployment (families)
	%	%
'A'	0.41	1.89
'B'	4.23	5.72
'C'	19.40	19.74
'D'	17.38	16.96
'E'	58.58	55.69

Then we made similar calculations, but drawing out of the pile every tenth schedule, thus showing what the situation would be if 10% of the heads of households were unemployed. This would represent a fairly severe degree of unemployment, and the results of our calculations on this basis are set out in the following table:

Class	Actual situation in 1950 (families)	Situation in 1950 with 10% unemployment (families)
	%	%
'A'	0.41	3.43
'B'	4.23	7.12
'C'	19.40	20.05
'D'	17.38	16.50
'E'	58.58	52.90

Finally, to obtain the best possible comparison with 1936, we made random selections from our schedules on such a scale as to represent the situation which would arise if 8.8% of the heads of households were unemployed. We chose this figure as being the actual level of unemployment in York in 1936. The result of these calculations is shown in the following table:

Class	Actaul situation in 1950 (families)	Situation in 1950 if unemployment had been at same level as 1936 (families)
	%	%
'A'	0.41	2.64
'B'	4.23	6.47
'C'	19.40	19.94
'D'	17.38	16.80
'E'	58.58	54.15

It will be seen from this table that if unemployment in York in 1950 had been at the same level as in 1936, 9.11% of working-class families would have been in poverty. In these families there were 4,934 individuals, equivalent to 7.85% of the working-class population. In 1936 31.1% of the working-class population were in poverty.

We see no reason why the three foregoing tables should not represent with a high degree of accuracy what the situation would be in our three hypothetical cases, but if unemployment were at all prolonged various factors would operate which would tend to upset our calculations. The principal of these factors are:

(a) The situation would be worsened in the case of the considerable proportion of families where payments became due on the hire purchase of furniture, or to building societies for the purchase of a house. We have no information about the former of these, except that we have evidence that many young couples make such payments, but we refer to the payments to building societies in Chapter 10. They are an important factor in the budgets of many families. The size of the instalments varies considerably, but £2 8s. a month is about the minimum, to which must be added rates, and the cost of repairs and maintenance.

(b) Many families renting dwellings, particularly those in the more expensive council houses, would no doubt give them up in a time of prolonged unemployment and would live more cheaply with relatives or friends.

(c) School meals, for which, in all except the poorest families, children are made to pay at a rate of 2s. 6d. per week, would no doubt be given free to those whose fathers were in poverty through unemployment.

(d) Substantial unemployment of the heads of households would probably reduce the number of women who have taken jobs to supplement their husbands' earnings. We examine the question of women at work in Chapter 7. Their withdrawal in a time of general unemployment would obviously have an adverse effect on the situation as we found it in 1950.

(e) As explained in Chapter 2, our poverty line income includes allowances for clothing and for household sundries. Except in long periods of unemployment, many of these purchases could be postponed without any serious effects, in order to allow the available income to be concentrated on the most essential items of expenditure.

On the whole we conclude, as a result of our examination of the situation as it would be in the event of (a) slight and (b) moderately severe unemployment, that although the development of welfare legislation since 1936 has certainly not ensured that men can normally be unemployed without their families falling into poverty, it has, both by the National Insurance Act itself, and by the other welfare measures, substantially reduced the amount and the severity of the poverty that would be consequent on unemployment.

CHAPTER SIX

INDUSTRIAL PENSIONS

We turn now to an examination of the question of industrial pensions, including in that term any pensions that are earned by a long period of employment, even though the employment may not actually have been in industry. We also include pensions earned by virtue of contributions to friendly societies. All these pensions are, of course, additional to any retirement pensions paid under the National Insurance Act, with which we are not concerned in this chapter.

1,242 persons among the working-class families of York are in receipt of industrial pensions, and the sources of these are as follows:

Industrial and trading concerns (including Co-operative Society)	477
British Railways	306
Civil Service, Teachers, Police, and City Corporation	288
Armed Forces	135
Friendly Societies	36

We are unable to say with complete certainty in how may cases the recipient of the pension contributed during his or her working life towards the fund out of which it is paid, but this is certainly so in a majority of cases, probably in approximately two-thirds of the whole. Where a pension is contributory, participation is usually (but not always) voluntary, and it follows that, even where pension schemes exist, a proportion of workers retire without a pension because in their youth they have either not wished, or have sometimes been too poor, to pay the contributions, or because they ceased to work for an employer operating a pension scheme.

The amounts of the pensions vary from trifling sums to sums large enough to support the recipient, and a wife if he has one, at a standard well above the poverty line, even if he has no other resources. The distribution of the 1,242 pensions according to size is as follows:

Less than 10s. a week	225
From 10s. 1d. to £1 0s. 0d. a week ..	234
From £1 0s. 1d. to £1 10s. 0d. a week ..	207
From £1 10s. 1d. to £2 0s. 0d. a week ..	90
From £2 0s. 1d. to £2 10s. 0d. a week ..	243
From £2 10s. 1d. to £3 0s. 0d. a week ..	144
Over £3 0s. 0d. a week	99

The pensioners are distributed among the five classes, 'A' to 'E', as follows:

'A'	18
'B'	99
'C'	459
'D'	378
'E'	288

The following table shows the relation between the amount of the pension and the class of the recipient:

Class	Amount of pension						
	Up to 10s.	10s. 1d. to 20s.	20s. 1d. to 30s.	30s. 1d. to 40s.	40s. 1d. to 50s.	50s. 1d. to 60s.	Over 60s.
'A'	—	—	—	—	18	—	—
'B'	54	18	9	—	9	9	—
'C'	135	90	90	27	54	27	36
'D'	36	72	72	36	81	54	27
'E'	—	54	36	27	81	54	36

We have examined the effect of industrial pensions on poverty by calculating from our schedules what changes there would be in the number of families in each class if there had been no industrial pensions but if every other circumstance had remained unaltered. The result of these calculations is given in the following table:

Class	Actual situation in 1950	Situation in 1950 if there had been no industrial pensions
	%	%
'A'	0.41	3.29
'B'	4.23	5.77
'C'	19.40	18.10
'D'	17.38	15.47
'E'	58.58	57.37

In considering this table two factors should, however, be taken into consideration. First, that a proportion of the persons reduced to poverty by the removal of their industrial pensions would in fact receive supplementary pensions from the Assistance Board ("supplementary" to their retirement pensions under the National Insurance Act), and would thus be raised above the poverty line. Second, since the great majority of industrial pensions are contributory, it is reasonable to suppose that a part of the individuals' contributions to the pension fund would have been set aside by the persons concerned as a provision for their old age, even if no pension scheme existed; this, too, would tend to reduce the increase of poverty that would follow the abolition of industrial pensions.

Despite the two mitigating factors to which we have just referred, our calculations nevertheless demonstrate that industrial pensions play an important part even in the Welfare State. Indeed, a comparison of the tables on pages 48 and 52 shows that the abolition of industrial pensions would create almost exactly the same amount of poverty as would follow if unemployment rose to the level (8.8%) it attained in 1936.

CHAPTER SEVEN

WOMEN AT WORK

On the whole the practice of women going out to work has, except in time of war, traditionally been restricted to widows, spinsters, and wives living apart from their husbands. This was the state of affairs in 1936 when "Poverty and Progress" was written, for B. S. Rowntree's second survey of York showed that, apart from the categories already mentioned, only an insignificant handful of women supplemented their husbands' earnings by going out to work.

Since 1936, however, the situation has changed in three respects. First, there is now virtually no unemployment. Second, large increases in the prices of clothing and household sundries have in many cases been accompanied by a considerable decline in quality so that housekeeping has become very expensive. Third, the fact that, on the whole, the working class is more prosperous than it has ever been, has created a desire in many families for goods that would formerly have been rejected without consideration as being entirely beyond their means. All these factors have combined to induce many women to go out to work even though their husbands are in full-time employment.

At the time of our investigation in 1950 the head of the household in 12,708 out of the 18,099 working-class families in York was a married man in full employment. The remainder consisted of retired persons, widows, spinsters, bachelors, widowers, and a few sick or disabled men. In 1,278 of the 12,708 households where the man was in full employment the wife was also in full, or part-time employment. The division of the working wives between our five Classes 'A' to 'E' is shown in the following table:

Class	Number of households with employed male as head	Number of wives working	
		Full time	Part time
'A'	27	—	9
'B'	54	—	18
'C'	1,341	—	36
'D'	2,001	18	108
'E'	9,285	171	918

It is significant that it is only by virtue of the wives' earnings that twenty-seven of the thirty-six families in Class 'C' escape poverty, for if the housewife did not work they would be in Class 'A'. Similarly, in Class 'D' the eighteen women who work full time are responsible for keeping their families out of poverty, for they would otherwise be in Class 'B', and twenty-seven further Class 'D' families would be in poverty (Class 'B') but for the part-time work of the housewife. On the other hand, of the 1,089 women in Class 'E' who are in full or part-time employment only forty-five of them are keeping their families out of poverty, and in the case of no less than 729 of them the family would be in Class 'E' without any income from the housewife.

Thus, among the working class of York as a whole, if no women went to work where the head of the household was an employed male, there would be 117 more families in poverty, thirty-six of them in Class 'A' and eighty-one in Class 'B'. The effect of this is shown in the following table:

Class	Actual		If no women worked	
	Families	%	Families	%
'A'	81	0.41	117	0.65
'B'	765	4.23	846	4.67
'C'	3,510	19.40	3,483	19.28
'D'	3,141	17.38	3,096	17.10
'E'	10,602	58.58	10,557	58.30

It is interesting to note that of the 1,278 women who go out to work 558 have no children under the age of 15, 288 have one child, 243 have two children, 108 have three, and 81 have four children or more.

Another matter worth mentioning is that 153 of the women who go out to work are aged between 20 and 29, 423 between 30 and 39, 477 between 40 and 49, and 225 are 50 or over.

We have made an analysis based on our investigators' reports of the reasons why women go out to work. We do not claim that it is absolutely accurate, but we believe it to be substantially so. It shows that 171 did so to enable them to buy furniture, etc., for the home, twenty-seven to pay for children's education, eighteen, most of whom were qualified nurses, did so from a sense of duty, 441 "to make ends meet", 351 to buy luxuries, and 270 for the pleasure of meeting other people instead of being cooped up in their homes all day.

The fact that a considerable number of those who would be in Classes 'D' and 'E' even if the women did not go out to work find it difficult to make ends meet, is a reflection on their housekeeping skill. For example, one woman with no children or dependent relatives, whose husband is earning £6 18s. net per week, told our investigator, "I just can't make the money go round, even though we both gave up smoking". In another house where the husband earned £8 2s. 6d. net and two grown-up children contributed £1 each and there were no dependent children or relatives, the wife said, "I've got to go out to work now with things the price they are. Even with my money we're always spent out by Thursday".

Many other women say frankly that they want a higher standard of living and are prepared to work to obtain it. Examples of the aims of these women are to buy a car, to have holidays away from York, to buy a radiogram, and to buy an electric machine for washing clothes or dishes.

Summary

Since 1936 a substantial number of working-class women, probably some 10% of all those who are married and with husbands in full employment, have formed the habit of taking paid employment to supplement the family income. This habit appears to be especially prevalent among the best-off sections of the working class. Although in a few cases it has the effect of raising the standard of a family which would otherwise have been in poverty, its main economic effects are to counteract the lack of skill of some housewives in spending their resources, and to enable working-class families to enjoy luxuries that would otherwise be beyond their means. An important proportion of women going to work, probably rather more than 20% of them, are actuated mainly by a desire to meet other people and thus to lead a less restricted life. This is a sociological fact which may prove to be of significance, but its discussion is outside the scope of this book.

Before passing on to consider other matters reference may be made to the fact that Richard Titmuss, in calling attention to certain contemporary family problems, has recently said, "It is a remarkable fact that in the so-called Welfare State there are more married women aged twenty-five to fifty-five at work outside the home than in any peace-time year during the past half-century. Compared with the situation in 1937, the number employed in factories, offices and shops may well have risen by 200 to 300 per cent."*

With a view to checking this estimate we have taken a random sample of 1,000 of the 1936 schedules of families where the male householder was in full-time employment and find that in only thirty-two cases, equal to 3.2% of the whole, did the wife go out to work, as compared with 10% in 1950.

* Broadcast in the Third Programme and reproduced in "The Listener" of the 1 5th March, 1951, page 411.

CHAPTER EIGHT

LIFE BELOW THE MINIMUM

In this chapter and the next one we give descriptions of what life is like in each of the Classes 'A' to 'E', and we are concerned first with life below the minimum, that is with Classes 'A' and 'B'.

As stated in Chapter 3, the percentages of working-class families in these classes are respectively 0.41% and 4.23%, and the total number of persons in them is 1,746. Even though this number is only one-tenth of the number (17,185) in 1936, it is still sufficiently large to represent a good deal of human suffering.

It will be remembered that the income limits of the two classes, after paying rent, are, Class 'A' under £3 17s. 2d., and Class 'B' from £3 17s. 2d. to £5 0s. 1d. In each case these sums are for a man, wife, and three children, and there are, of course, corresponding limits for larger or smaller families.

Since our poverty line is a stringent one and itself represents, as we fully recognise, a standard of living that is a good deal below what is desirable, and since Classes 'A' and 'B' fall below our poverty line, it follows that the 846 families in York in those classes are going short of the necessities of life, even if they did not spend anything on non-essentials.

We think that the best way to give an impression of life in Classes 'A' and 'B' is to give a number of extracts from our investigators' schedules, and these we give accordingly below. The fact that so many of these examples are of old people is, of course, a reflection of the fact stated in Chapter 3 that old age is the greatest contemporary cause of poverty and accounted for 68.1% of all the poverty in York in 1950.

In our examples, the figure for the total income includes all sums that the householder receives in cash or kind, including such welfare benefits as that derived from the provision of cheap milk for infants. The figure for "Deficit per head" is the amount by which the total resources of the family, after paying rent, fall short of the minimum income of the class, divided by the number of persons for whose maintenance the head of the household is responsible.

CLASS 'A'

1272   Three rooms, no bathroom. Own house. Rates 2s. 8d. per week. Widower aged 76 lives alone. Total income £1 6s. Deficit 14s. 7d. Just manages to keep going from week to week. Buys his rations and 1 oz. of tobacco per week (at the specially cheap rate for old age pensioners). No money for any other pleasures nor for replacements of clothes or household goods. Boot repairs are a great worry; when they have to be paid for he goes without his tobacco for several weeks.

1541   Six rooms and bathroom. Rent and rates £1 5s. 7d. Man 63, wife 62. Civil Service pension £2 8s. 10d. Value of home-grown vegetables 2s. 6d. Total income £2 11s. 4d. Deficit per head 15s. 4d. Man has only recently retired, and standard of living has not yet been adjusted. They are very much afraid they will have to give up their home, but have so far been unable to find a smaller house. They are well fitted up at present with clothes, but the man says, "These will have to last until I die. I shall never be able to afford any more".

1953   Six rooms and bathroom. Rent and rates
       16s. 5d. Man 44, wife 35, one son aged 10,
       two daughters aged 5 and 3. Man suffers from
       valvular disease of the heart and cannot work.
       He receives £1 13s. 6d. a week health insurance.
       Wife works as a part-time barmaid and receives
       £2. Family allowances 10s. Value of school
       milk and cheap milk 3s. 3d. Two elder children
       receive free dinners at school, the value being
       3s. 10d. per week. Total income £4 10s. 7d.
       Deficit 5s. 3d. per head. Wife says it is impos-
       sible to manage on the money, her chief worry
       being the provision of clothes for the children.
       The husband hopes to be able to work again
       soon, but will only be able to do a light job.

CLASS 'B'

734   Four rooms, no bathroom. Rent and rates
       8s. Spinster aged 87. Old age pension of
       £1 6s. is sole income. Deficit 15s. 6d. Very
       lonely and unhappy, although neighbours help
       with her housework. Cannot buy the necessities
       of life, and does not know what to do.

993   Three rooms, no bathroom. Rent and rates
       8s. 3d. Widower 85 and invalid daughter 50.
       Old age pension £1 6s., allowance for daughter
       £1 6s. Value of home-grown vegetables 2s. 6d.
       Total income £2 14s. 6d. Deficit 3s. 11d. per
       head. Although they still suffer considerable
       privation (for example they can only afford
       half a pint of milk per day) their main feeling is
       gratitude for the welfare legislation, before the
       passing of which they lived on 17s. 6d. per
       week between them, nearly half of which went
       in rent and rates.

1273   Three rooms, no bathroom. Own house. Rates 2s. 10d. per week. Spinster of 76 with no income other than old age pension of £1 6s. Deficit 7s. 11d. per week. Spinster very lonely and, owing to age, is not able to cope very well with her problems. House very dirty. Scraps of food, soiled crockery and dirty clothing scattered about her living room. Has no money to buy clothes.

1007   Six rooms and bathroom. Rent and rates 17s. 8d. Man 42, wife 40. Five sons, aged 10, 8, 6, 5, and 3. Man is male nurse earning £5 16s. 5d. Family allowances £1. Value of school milk and cheap milk 4s. 9d. Value of home-grown vegetables 2s. 6d. Total income £7 3s. 8d. Deficit 4d. per head. Wife complains of great difficulty in paying for children's clothes, and of the cost of shoe repairs. Says she can hardly make ends meet and just doesn't know what she will do if prices rise.

741   Two rooms and kitchen. Rent and rates 8s. 3d. Widow aged 76 living alone. Old age pension £1 6s. Supplementary pension 8s. Value of home-grown vegetables 2s. 6d. Total income £1 16s. 6d. Deficit 5s. 2d. Widow says she concentrates her spending on food, even though she sometimes has to go without a fire in consequence. Shoe repairs are a big problem, but she has a good stock of clothes and hopes she won't live long enough to wear them out.

909   Six rooms and bathroom. Rent and rates 19s. 7d. Man 40, wife 31. Three sons, aged 9, 8, and 3, and four daughters aged 11, 5, 4, and 10 weeks. Man self-employed as general dealer, average net profit £5 10s. per week. Family

allowances £1 10s. Value of school milk and cheap milk 7s. 3d. Value of home-grown vegetables 2s. 6d. Total income £7 9s. 9d. Deficit per head 2s. 11d. Wife says they "just scrape along". She has to wash and iron every day and, apart from the work, this is a heavy expense in fuel and soap. No money for pleasure of any kind.

976   Five rooms and bathroom. Rent and rates 17s. Man 42, wife 37. Two sons aged 15 and 3, and two daughters aged 13 and 9. Man is unskilled labourer and earns £5 4s. Family allowances 15s. Value of school and cheap milk 4s. Value of home-grown vegetables 2s. 6d. Total income £6 5s. 6d. Deficit per head 1s. Wife complains that owing to high prices they cannot buy either enough food or adequate clothing. As an example she states that they can only afford 1½ pints of milk per day. When children's shoes have to be repaired the family have to economise still more on food. Husband complains of having to keep children at school until age of 15. He says that not only ought they to be earning, but that in their last year at school they demand pocket money. Through unskilled management this family probably suffers more than it need.

606   Two rooms and an attic. Rent and rates 8s. 7d. Widower aged 79. Old age pension £1 6s. Supplementary pension 8s. 6d. Chelsea Hospital pension 4s. Total income £1 18s. 6d. Deficit 8s. 3d. House has been condemned and is very damp. Widower has difficult time to make ends meet, but he keeps his house clean, and takes pride in his skill as a "washerwoman". His only luxury is 1 oz. of tobacco a week,

bought at the special concession price of 1s. 1½d. for old age pensioners. If faced with any extra expense, such as boot repairs, he goes without his food, but never without his 1 oz. of tobacco.

696   Six rooms, no bathroom. Own house, rates 4s. 7d. per week. Widower of 86. Industrial pension 8s. 1d. Old age pension £1 6s. Help from sons 10s. per week. Total income £2 4s. 1d. Deficit 9s. 5d. Widower nearly blind and because of arthritis can hardly walk. Has to pay 10s. a week to a charwoman and 1s. per week for hire of a wheel chair. Suffers greatly from cold and really needs a fire night and day, but this is impossible because of the cost. He says his children are very good to him, and, in addition to help in cash and with gifts of foodstuffs, he always has his Sunday dinner with them.

419   Four rooms, no bathroom. Rent and rates 12s. 3d. Man 79 and wife 80. Old age pension £2 2s. Supplementary pension 10s. 6d. Total income £2 12s. 6d. Deficit 8s. per head. Because they buy no clothes, they can just manage on their income, but there is no money for pleasure. They both suffer from the cold, and if they had any more money it would be spent on more coal in preference to anything else.

1472   Four rooms and bathroom. Buying house through building society; instalments plus rates amount to £1 11s. 4d. per week. Man 38, wife 35. One son aged 4. Man is an unskilled worker and earns £4 16s. Value of cheap milk 1s. 9d. Total income £4 17s. 9d. Deficit 1s. 10d.

per head. Wife is an exceptionally good manager, and this family live better than many in
Class 'C'. They even manage to have an annual
holiday away from home, and occasionally to
go to the cinema. The husband is a moderate
smoker. The secret of this "prosperous" household is no doubt self-denial by the wife.

657 Five rooms, no bathroom. Rent and rates
11s. 1d. Man 75 and wife 74. Industrial pension
8s. 2d. Old age pension £2 2s. Supplementary
pension 11s. 6d. Total income £3 1s. 8d.
Deficit 2s. 9d. per head. This old couple say
they "get along fairly well" because they never
buy any clothes, replenishments of which they
consider unnecessary at their age. They have
little money to spend on pleasures, but in the
summer they manage an occasional day trip to
the sea-side. They are undoubtedly protected
by the pension paid by the man's former
employer from the graver effects of poverty.

653 Six rooms, no bathroom. Own house; rates
3s. 2d. per week. Man 72 and wife 70. Male
lodger. Man receives retirement pension, but
as wife in unable to produce a birth certificate
(or to prove her date of birth in any other way)
she is ineligible for an old age pension and
receives national assistance in lieu. Man's
pension plus woman's national assistance amount
to £1 19s. Lodger pays £1 10s. Total income
£3 9s. Deficit 1s. 7d. per head (for man and
wife). This family manage fairly well although
there is no money except for essentials. A
proportion of the income is spent by the wife
on patent medicines which she considers
essential, and which are bought to the detri-
ment of more normal necessities.

That the number of persons in poverty has fallen between 1936 and 1950 from 17,185 to 1,746 is obviously in itself a cause of great satisfaction. But even these figures do not fully represent the improvement that has taken place, for a study of the examples given above shows that even when persons were in poverty in 1950 their suffering was less acute than that of persons in a corresponding position in 1936. This qualitative improvement is of course due primarily to the welfare measures that have alleviated poverty even when they have not been able to cure it.

CHAPTER NINE

LIFE ABOVE THE MINIMUM

We turn now to examine matters concerning families living above the poverty line, i.e., to Classes 'C', 'D', and 'E'.

As stated in Chapter 3, the percentages of working-class families in these categories are respectively 19.4%, 17.3%, and 58.5%, so that together they represent a large majority of the working class. It will be remembered that the income limits of the three classes, after paying rent, are, Class 'C' from £5 0s. 2d. to £6 3s. 1d., Class 'D' from £6 3s. 2d. to £7 6s. 1d., and Class 'E' £7 6s. 2d. and above. In each case these sums are for a man, wife and three children, and there are, of course, corresponding limits for larger and smaller families.

Although families in Class 'E' are in fairly comfortable circumstances, those in Class 'C', particularly the less well-off in the Class, are not far removed from poverty, and there is no doubt that they suffer a good deal of stringency. Unless they concentrate all their spending power on absolute necessities, they will suffer from the same evils of hunger and cold as are (at least to some extent) the lot of those in Classes 'A' and 'B'. In order to show how many persons in Class 'C' are near to the poverty line, we have divided all the persons in that Class into four groups according to their incomes. The difference in income between each group is 5s. 9d. (i.e., one-quarter of 23s.) in the case of a family of five, or the equivalent of this for larger or smaller families. When the 3,510 families in Class 'C' are divided in this way, we have:

Quartiles of Class 'C'	1950		1936
	No. of families	%	%
'C1' (lowest standard)	1,395	39.7	28.2
'C2'	711	20.3	25.5
'C3'	747	21.3	23.4
'C4'	657	18.7	22.9

From this table we see that 1,395 families, although they are above our poverty line, are nevertheless living in conditions so stringent as to be hardly better off than those who are just below it.

We thought it would also be of interest to divide Class 'D' into two income groups with a view to showing how many of the 3,141 families are living in conditions approximating to those of the hard-pressed families in Class 'C', and how many live in circumstances more nearly akin to those of the comparatively well-to-do families in Class 'E'.

We have accordingly divided the families into those with incomes of less and more respectively than 11s. 6d. above those in Class 'C'. (We refer, of course, to families of man, wife, and three children, or the equivalent of this for differently constituted families). We found that 1,828 families (58.2%) are living in the lower income half of the group, and 1,313 (41.8%) in the upper half.

It is, incidentally, possible, from the foregoing figures relating to Classes 'C' and 'D', for any reader who thinks that our poverty line is too stringent, and that accordingly our report about the amount of poverty we have found is too favourable, to ascertain for himself how much poverty there would be if the

poverty line were fixed at various income levels. For
example, if instead of being £5 0s. 2d. (or its equivalent)
it were £5 5s. 11d., the amount of poverty would be
determined by adding the number of families in Class
'C1' to those in Classes 'A' and 'B', and so on.

One of the matters we wished to examine in connection with life above our poverty line was whether
there was any consistent relation between a man's
employment and his economic class, for example
whether unskilled workers were usually in Class 'C'
and skilled in Class 'E'. We examined one hundred
schedules drawn at random from each of Classes 'C',
'D', and 'E', but could find no consistent relation
between class and employment. As an illustration we
give below the nature of the employment of ten men
in each of the three classes. These thirty were among
our random selection of 300 of which mention has
just been made.

Class 'C'	Class 'D'	Class 'E'
Lorry driver	Goods porter (B.R.)*	Lorry driver
Male nurse	Window cleaner	Male nurse
Brewer's labourer	Waiter	Upholsterer
General labourer	General labourer	Builder's labourer
Road sweeper	Grocer's assistant	Electrical fitter
Civil Service clerk	Civil Service clerk	Civil Service clerk
Commercial traveller	Sign writer	Railway clerk
Hairdresser	Hairdresser	Bricklayer
Bus conductor	Police constable	Postman
Engine driver (B.R.)	Fireman (B.R.)	Ticket collector (B.R.)

To give an impression of life in Classes 'C', 'D', and
'E', we follow the procedure adopted in the last
chapter when describing life in Classes 'A' and 'B', and
give a number of extracts from our investigators'
schedules. In these extracts the ages of female children
are printed in italics. The figure showing "Surplus per
head" is arrived at by dividing the surplus above the

* B.R. ━ British Railways.

minimum income of the class by the number of persons dependent on the householder. The minimum income of each class is:

For Class 'C', above £5 0s. 2d.　⎱ For a man, wife, and three dependent
For Class 'D', above £6 3s. 2d.　⎬ children, or the equivalent of that
For Class 'E', above £7 6s. 2d.　⎰ sum for differently constituted families.

CLASS 'C'*

1307　Four rooms, no bathroom. Rent and rates 11s. per week. Man 36, wife 34, children 6, 5, and 6 months. Man is shop assistant earning £5 6s. 8d. per week. Family allowances 10s. School milk and cheap milk (for infant) to value of 3s. 3d. per week. Total income £5 19s. 11d. Surplus 1s. 9d. per head. The wife stated she could barely manage on her income. They found it impossible to save, and have been unable to afford to go away for a holiday. Her main financial worry is the price of children's clothing. (*Second quartile*).

1974　Five rooms, no bathroom. Rent and rates £1 4s. per week. Man 37, wife 34, five children aged *10*, *8*, *6*, 6, and 5. Man works as a lorry driver and earns £5 10s. per week. Woman, working part time in an office, earns £1 10s. per week. Family allowances £1. School milk to a value of 3s. 9d. Vegetables grown on allotment to value of 7s. 6d. per week. Total income £8 11s. 3d. per week. Surplus 2s. 8d. per head. The wife stated that unless she went out to work she could not pay for the children's clothes. The family have no holidays away from home and cannot save. (*Third quartile*).

* At the end of each extract relating to a family in Class 'C' we indicate the appropriate quartile. The limits of these quartiles are referred to on page 67. The first quartile is the lowest and the fourth the highest within the Class.

508   Seven rooms, no bathroom. Rent and rates £1 0s. 10d. per week. Widow 47, two children aged *17* and 8, and two lodgers (not boarded). Widow works part time as waitress. Girl 17 works in a shop. Widow's earnings plus pension amount to £3 3s. 6d. Girl contributes 15s. and lodgers pay 7s. 6d. each. School milk to value of 9d. Total income £4 14s. 3d. Surplus 7s. 5d. per head. The widow says she lives hand-to-mouth and has "a pretty hard struggle to manage". (*Fourth quartile*).

1053   Four rooms and a shop, no bathroom. Rent and rates £1 0s. 3d. per week. Man 64, wife 58. They keep a small general store. Profit in a fair week amounts to about £4, and this is their total income. Surplus 1s. 3d. per head. Wife states that not infrequently profit from shop is insufficient for their needs and when this is so the husband finds casual work or, if unable to do so, registers as unemployed. (*First quartile*).

1115   Five rooms and bathroom. Own house, rates 4s. per week. Spinster 56, her niece 40 (separated from husband), niece's child *3*, and a male lodger. Niece pays £2 per week for herself and the child, and the lodger £1 12s. 6d. Cheap milk for the child to value of 1s. 3d. Total income £3 13s. 9d. Surplus 1s. 7d. per head. Householder complains of hard struggle to make both ends meet. (*Second quartile*).

1295   Four rooms, no bathroom. Rent and rates 14s. 1d. The house is dark and dirty and has been condemned. Man 35, woman 34. Four children 13, *7*, *5*, and 2. Man has own business as general dealer in scrap. Average profit £5 10s. Family allowances 15s. School milk and cheap milk to value of 4s. Total income £6 9s. Surplus 1d. per head. Another child expected shortly when family will drop to Class 'B'. (*First quartile*).

1389 Four rooms, no bathroom. Rent and rates 8s. 11d. Man 40, woman 31, three children *11*, *9*, and *8*. Man is a dairy-roundsman and earns £5 8s. 6d. Family allowances 10s. School milk to value of 2s. 3d. Total income £6 0s. 9d. Surplus 2s. 4d. per head. Wife says the family is "Just scraping along". She considers her husband is underpaid, having regard to present day prices, particularly of children's clothing. (*Third quartile*).

1492 Three rooms, scullery and bathroom. Rent and rates £1 1s. 6d. Man 31, woman 24, one child *2*. Man is a student male nurse and receives £4 13s. 6d. per week. Cheap milk to the value of 1s. 9d. Most of vegetables home grown to estimated net value of 5s. per week. Total income £5 0s. 3d. Surplus 2s. 3d. per head. Wife states that financial position is very difficult as they pay £1 per week on hire purchase of furniture. Wife formerly had an insurance policy, but had to surrender it to buy clothes for daughter. Husband remains on present rate of pay for another two years. (*Second quartile*).

1635 Five rooms and bathroom. Rent and rates 19s. 1d. Widow 57, married daughter 21, son-in-law 23. Widow receives pension of 10s. and earns another £1 as a part-time cleaner. Daughter and son-in-law pay £2 15s. for full board. Total income £4 5s. Surplus 11s. 2d. (widow only). Hire purchase of furniture £3 7s. per month. Widow cannot afford a holiday and the hire purchase uses up so much of her income that she is very short of money. (*Fourth quartile*).

1671   Six rooms, no bathroom. Rent and rates 11s. 1d. Man 34, woman 31, four children aged 8, 4, 2½, and 6 months. Man is a railway worker and receives £6 9s. 4d. Family allowances 15s. Value of school milk and cheap milk 5s. 9d. Total income £7 10s. 1d. Surplus 4s. 1d. per head. Man and wife complain they are unable to make ends meet. They are in debt and at regular intervals seek help from man's parents. Wife's mother makes most of clothing for younger children. Cannot afford dinners at school for eldest child (these cost 2s. 6d. per week). Spend no money on amusements, and going away for holidays is out of the question. Only luxury is husband's smoking (twenty or thirty cigarettes a week). (*Third quartile*).

CLASS 'D'

1988   Six rooms and bathroom. Rent and rates 25s. 2d. Man 28, wife 27, five children 10, 7, 5, 2½, and 7 months. Man works in factory (confectionery) and earns £6 9s. 5d. Wife works half time in same factory £1 16s. 4d. Family allowances £1. Man is member of Royal Naval Volunteer Reserve and receives quarterly retainer equivalent to 8s. 6d. per week. Value of school milk and cheap milk 5s. 3d. Value of home-grown vegetables 2s. 6d. Total income £10 2s. Surplus 6s. 10d. per head. Wife complains of the high cost of clothing and of the high rent. She says that without her earnings they could not make ends meet.

9   Four rooms, no bathroom. Rent and rates 17s. 6d. Widow "over 65" living alone. Works full time (domestic work) and earns £2 14s. 8d. in addition to pension of 10s. Total income £3 4s. 8d. Surplus 11s. 1d. Has been widow over twenty years. Enjoys her work because of the companionship it brings her. Complains of high rent.

711   Four rooms, no bathroom. Rent and rates 9s. 6d. Widow 62. Man (widow's brother) 79. Widow's pension £1 6s. War pension to widow for son killed £1. Brother pays £1 5s. for full board. Total income £3 11s. Surplus (widow only) 17s. 3d. Widow states that they "manage fairly comfortably".

368   Nine rooms and bathroom. Rent and rates £1 10s. 4d. Man 40, wife 38, two children aged 9 and 6, two lodgers. Man is electrician and earns £6 1s. 7d. Family allowance 5s., value of school milk 1s. 6d. Lodgers pay £1 10s. each for full board. Total income £9 8s. 1d. Surplus 11s. 5d. per head. Wife complains of high cost of living. They cannot save nor go away for holidays. They can afford very little for amusements.

942   Four rooms and bathroom (house is a "prefab"). Rent and rates 19s. 9d. Man 35, wife 32. Two children 8 and 1. Man is electrician and earns £6 1s. 6d. Family allowance 5s. Value of home-grown vegetables 3s. 9d. Value of school milk and cheap milk 2s. 6d. Total income £6 12s. 9d. Surplus 6s. 6d. per head. Wife says that all the money coming in has to be spent on necessities and there is nothing for saving or pleasure. Husband used to smoke and

drink in moderation, but has given up both as he cannot afford them. Has to meet a coal bill of £2 and has no money to pay it. Thinks rent is excessive.

755 Five rooms and bathroom. Buying house through building society. Instalments plus rates are equivalent to £1 7s. 5d. per week. Man 41, wife 30. One child aged 5. Man is Civil Service clerk and earns £6 8s. 9d. Value of school milk 9d. Total income £6 9s. 6d. Surplus 10s. 1d. per head. Complains of cost of children's clothing, but they can afford an annual holiday and spend up to 10s. per week on pleasure. No saving apart from buying house.

802 Five rooms and bathroom. Rent and rates 15s. per week. Man 50, wife 38, four children aged *18*, *17*, 14, and 8. Man is railway worker and earns £5 14s. Two eldest children are at work and contribute £1 each per week. Family allowance 5s. Value of school milk 1s. 6d. Value of home-grown vegetables 2s. 6d. Total income £8 3s. Surplus 6s. 8d. per head. Wife says they "manage well enough now, but it was a terrible struggle when the children were young and there were no family allowances". They spend their annual holiday in day trips.

1524 Five rooms and bathroom. Rent and rates 14s. 7d. per week. Spinster 59. Four lodgers (all relatives of householder). Only source of income is contributions of the lodgers and these total £5 14s. per week, giving the spinster a surplus of 19s. She says that she has "no financial difficulties, though money is by no means plentiful".

793   Five rooms and bathroom. Rent and rates
        16s. 3d. Man 37, wife 40, three children aged
        14, 11, and 9. Man is railway worker and
        earns £7 10s. 1d. Family allowances 10s.
        Value of school milk 2s. 3d. Total income
        £8 2s. 4d. Surplus 9s. 1d. per head. Wife com-
        plains that family income is inadequate for
        maintenance of three children and she is looking
        for part-time work. They are short of some
        near-necessities of household equipment (e.g.,
        no floor covering on the stairs). They save
        regularly, however, to pay for an annual
        holiday.

1669   Six rooms, no bathroom. Rent and rates
        14s. 11d. Man 36, wife 35, four children *12*,
        7, *5*, and 3, and three male lodgers. Man is
        railway worker and earns £5 4s. 4d. Family
        allowances 15s. Value of school milk and
        cheap milk 4s. Total payments from lodgers
        £5 5s. for full board. Total income £11 8s. 4d.
        Surplus 10s. 1d. per head (family only). Wife
        complains of cost of children's clothing. Finds
        work of three lodgers in addition to own family
        a very heavy burden, but couldn't possibly
        make ends meet without all three of them.

CLASS 'E'

828   Five rooms, no bathroom. Rent and rates
        9s. 11d. Man 56, wife 56. Man is bill-poster
        and earns £5 6s. which is total family income,
        giving surplus of 19s. 5d. per head. Wife says
        they live quietly but have no difficulties. Are
        able to go away for an annual holiday, spend a
        reasonable amount on pleasure and still save a
        bit for their old age.

551   Four rooms, no bathroom. Rent and rates
       12s. per week. Man 47, wife 42. One child
       aged 7. Man is a machinist at a factory power
       plant and earns £7 6s. 1d. Value of school milk
       9d. Value of home-grown vegetables 5s. Total
       income £7 11s. 10d. Surplus £1 2s. 3d. per head.
       Wife very cheerful and happy. No financial
       problems.

15   Five rooms and bathroom. Rent and rates
       £1 3s. 4d. per week. Man 44, wife 51. Two
       children aged 16 and 13. One male lodger.
       Man is railway worker and earns £9 5s. 3d.
       Family allowance 5s. Value of school milk
       1s. 6d. Value of home-grown vegetables 2s. 6d.
       Lodger pays £2 2s. Total income £11 16s. 3d.
       Surplus £1 8s. 2d. per head. Family circum-
       stances very good. House is fitted with telephone.
       Elder son goes to a boarding school. Parents
       hope it may be possible for both children to
       go to a University.

2018   Five rooms and bathroom. Rent and rates
       16s. 5d. per week. Man 44, wife 39. Three
       children 16, 12, and 4. Man is railway worker
       and earns £7 2s. 8d. Wife works part-time in
       factory for £2. Eldest child is an apprentice
       and contributes 15s. to family income. Family
       allowance 5s. Value of school milk and cheap
       milk 2s. 6d. Total income £10 5s. 2d. Surplus
       17s. 10d. per head. Wife says she has a hard
       struggle to make ends meet, and they could
       not do so without her earnings, though her
       absence at work means that the child aged 4
       has to be sent to a day nursery.

1473   Four rooms and bathroom. Own house. Rates
       4s. 5d. per week. Man 44, wife 40. Three
       children *20*, *7*, and *5*. Man is a journeyman

baker and earns £7 17s. 3d. Eldest girl contributes £1 10s. to family income. Family allowance 5s. Value of vegetables grown 7s. 6d. Value of school milk 1s. 6d. Total income £10 1s. 3d. Surplus 19s. 11d. per head. Wife makes all clothes of two younger children and most of her own. She finds it difficult to manage on the family income. No saving and they spend their annual holiday in day trips because it is cheaper than going away.

1734   Four rooms, no bathroom. Rent and rates 9s. 6d. Man 46, wife 45. Five children 24, 17, *13*, *10*, and 4. Man is an engine driver, and earns £8 1s. 8d. Two elder children contribute £1 18s. each. Family allowances 10s. Value of vegetables grown 7s. 6d. Value of school milk and cheap milk 3s. 3d. Total income £12 18s. 5d. Surplus 17s. 6d. per head. House is too small for number of people in it. Wife says she can manage, but it's very difficult to save. She complains of the amount of work she has to do, particularly a weekly wash for seven people, and wishes she could afford to send some of the washing to a laundry.

1907   Four rooms, no bathroom. Own house. Rates 3s. per week. Man 40, wife 30. Two children aged *3* and 6 months. Man is a railway worker and earns £7 8s. 1d. Family allowance 5s. Cheap milk to value of 3s. 6d. Total income £7 16s. 7d. Surplus 16s. 10d. per head. Wife says they can only just manage, but they are able to have an annual holiday which they spend in a caravan.

826   Six rooms and bathroom. Own house. Rates 4s. 7d. per week. Man 35, wife 35. Three children *8*, 7, and 4. Man is an electrician and earns £8 9s. 11d. Family allowances 10s.

Value of school milk and cheap milk 3s. 3d.
Value of home-grown vegetables 5s. Total
income £9 8s. 2d. Surplus 12s. 8d. per head
Wife is a good manager and this family is quite
prosperous and contented. They have an 8 h.p.
motor car.

800   Five rooms and bathroom. Rent and rates
15s. 2d. per week. Man 44, wife 40. Five
children, aged 18, 17, *13*, 9, and 6. Man is
railway worker and earns £6 3s. 4d. Wife
works part-time in a factory and earns £2 3s. 3d.
Two elder children contribute £2 19s. Family
allowances 10s. Value of school milk 2s. 3d.
Value of home-grown vegetables 2s. 6d. Total
income £12 0s. 4d. Surplus 14s. 2d. per head.
Wife complains that unless she earns they
cannot make ends meet. They occasionally
manage a holiday in a caravan which they
borrow from the wife's mother.

1373   Four rooms, no bathroom. Rent and rates
9s. 3d. per week. Man 32, wife 33. Three
children aged 11, *8*, and *3*. Man works in a
factory (confectionery) and earns £6 7s. 2d.
Wife works part-time as a shop assistant and
earns £1 11s. 11d. Family allowances 10s.
Value of school milk and cheap milk 3s. 3d.
Total income £8 12s. 4d. Surplus 12s. 6d. per
head. Wife complains of the cost of children's
clothes, and says that though they manage to
save a little and to go away for holidays, they
have to be careful.

There is one important matter to which we wish to
refer briefly in this chapter, and that is to point out
that although our investigations show the state of
affairs in York at a given time, and although there is no
reason to believe (apart from definite changes in

conditions) that the picture would be different at any other time, the conditions of individual families change appreciably over a lifetime, and they pass from class to class. The reason for this becomes clear if we consider a hypothetical family, the Smiths.

If the Smiths are married when he is aged 30 and she is 25, and he is earning £5 10s. net per week, and they pay 15s. rent and rates, they will be in Class 'E' on marriage. On the birth of their first child they drop to Class 'D'. On the birth of the second child they drop to Class 'C'. With the birth of a third child they remain in Class 'C', and—if there are no more children—they stay there until the first child goes to work and contributes to the costs of the home. As successive children go to work, the Smiths ascend once more to Class 'E', and enjoy a number of years of prosperity. When Mr. Smith reaches the age of 65, and if he ceases to earn, and unless he has substantial savings, which is unlikely, he and his wife enter another period of decline. When any savings they may have are spent, they drop from 'E', through 'D' to 'C'. At the rates of retirement pensions in force in 1950 at the time of our investigations (but subsequently increased in the Budget in 1951) the Smiths would have fallen into poverty for the first time in their lives, and they would—except perhaps for help given by their children—have ended their existence in Classes 'A' or 'B'. At the new (1951) rate of retirement pensions, they would remain above the poverty line, in the lowest quartile of Class 'C'.

It follows that although the proportions of the working class in Classes 'A', 'B', and 'C' at any given time are those shown in the table at the end of Chapter 3, and elsewhere in this book, the proportion who suffer the poverty of Classes 'A' and 'B', or the severe stringency of Class 'C', at some time in their lives is very much higher.

CHAPTER TEN

HOUSING

There are 29,900 houses in York, of which 18,099 are working-class houses within our definition of the term working class, i.e., families where the earnings of the chief wage earner do not exceed £550 per annum. In deciding whether a family is "working class" we are concerned only with earnings, so that we include many families where the chief wage earner is a clerical worker or even a member of one of the less well paid professions. The total number of houses in the city is made up as follows:

(a)   Unsatisfactory houses, for the demolition of which provision has been made in the City's scheme of slum clearance prepared under the Town and Country Planning Act, 1947   5,966

(b)   Satisfactory houses built before 1920   13,091

(c)   Houses built since 1920, both by the Local Authority and by private enterprise, and situated in new estates or residential suburbs   10,843

                                       29,900

The 5,966 houses that are unsatisfactory will, in accordance with the provisions of the Town and Country Planning Act, 1947, be replaced in four groups over a period of twenty years. Each group will be dealt with in a period of five years, as follows:

First five year period	1,659 houses
Second five year period	1,518 houses
Third five year period	1,453 houses
Fourth five year period	1,336 houses
	5,966 houses

The 1,659 houses scheduled to be dealt with in the first of the five year periods referred to above include all the houses in York that can for any reason (such as the decay of the structure, or the absence of water laid on in the house) be described as slum properties. The houses scheduled for attention in the subsequent five year periods are those which are in quite tolerable condition at present, but which are likely to deteriorate within the periods of years indicated, so that they will no longer be up to the minimum acceptable standard.

Sanitation

A large majority of houses in York have their own water closets, but 1,589 houses still have waste-water closets, of the type known locally as "ducketts" and these are considered by the City Health Authorities to be thoroughly unsatisfactory. At the time of B. S. Rowntree's survey of York in 1936, there were 2,204 such houses.

Water supply

York enjoys a good supply of cheap water, the water rate of an average working-class house with a bathroom and one water closet being only about 4d. a week. With few exceptions every house has its own internal piped water supply.

Bathrooms

Of the 18,099 working-class houses 48.5% have no bathrooms. Although, as might be expected, a larger proportion of the better off among the working class have bathrooms than is the case with those below or near the poverty line, nevertheless many quite well-to-do working-class families have to do without what is now regarded as a near-necessity. The division of Classes 'A' to 'E' of the working class according to whether or not they live in houses with bathrooms is given in the following table:

Class	Number of families with a bathroom	Number of families without a bathroom
'A'	36	45
'B'	216	549
'C'	1,575	1,935
'D'	1,584	1,557
'E'	5,895	4,707
Total	9,306	8,793

Number of families living in council houses

Of the 29,900 houses in York, 6,212 have been built by the Local Authority. These are always referred to as council houses. There are also 449 temporary bungalows, delivered prefabricated to the selected sites and erected by the Local Authority. The remaining 23,239 houses have been built by private enterprise, usually for sale either to owner-occupiers, or to the considerable number of persons who like house property as an investment.

Of the 6,212 council houses and 449 prefabricated bungalows (usually known simply as "pre-fabs", a term we use in this chapter), 5,697 and 432 respectively are occupied by working-class families. 515 council houses and seventeen pre-fabs are occupied by families in which the earnings of the chief wage earner are above the figure we have taken in defining the term "working class".

The distribution by Classes 'A' to 'E' of the 18,099 working-class families of York among houses of different types is shown in the following table:

Class	Number of families living in		
	Council houses	Pre-fabs	Private enterprise houses
'A'	27	—	54
'B'	279	—	486
'C'	1,422	36	2,052
'D'	1,179	126	1,836
'E'	2,790	270	7,542
Total	5,697	432	11,970

Owner-occupiers

Of the 18,099 working-class families in York, 4,005 own the houses they occupy, and a further 1,125 are still in the process of buying them through building societies. The following table shows how the owner-occupiers, actual and partial, are divided between Classes 'A' to 'E'.

Class	Number of families owning the house they occupy	Number of families buying the house they occupy through a building society
'A'	18	9
'B'	99	18
'C'	576	135
'D'	558	180
'E'	2,754	783
Total	4,005	1,125

We do not know how many of the 4,005 owners have a mortgage on their houses. This was not a question which the investigators could suitably ask.

Rent and rates

Since among the working classes of York there are, as stated above, 5,130 families owning or buying their houses, it follows that the remaining 12,969 families live in houses owned by somebody else. In the large majority of cases rent is paid to the owners of the houses, although a small minority of families live rent free, usually in houses owned by a close relative.

The following table shows what sums are paid each week in rent and rates by persons in each of the Classes 'A' to 'E':

Class	Number of families paying rent and rates amounting to					
	None at all	10s. and under	10s. 1d. to 15s.	15s. 1d. to 20s.	20s. 1d. to 25s.	Over 25s.
'A'	—	—	27	18	—	9
'B'	27	333	144	135	9	—
'C'	36	729	846	711	387	81
'D'	—	504	792	684	279	153
'E'	27	1,044	2,421	2,439	828	306
Total	90	2,610	4,230	3,987	1,503	549

Where rents are paid, these vary greatly, even between houses with the same number of rooms. In these circumstances average figures for the rents of houses of different sizes would be meaningless, but in the following table we show both the range of rents and our estimate of the rent most frequently paid:

Size of house	Range of rent	A normal rent
Six rooms and a bathroom ..	10s. to 25s.	18s. 6d.
Six rooms without a bathroom	10s. to 18s.	14s.
Five rooms and a bathroom ..	11s. to 20s.	14s.
Five rooms without a bathroom	7s. to 12s.	10s.
Four rooms without a bathroom	7s. to 10s.	7s. 6d.
Pre-fab (four rooms and a bath-room)	19s. 9d.	19s. 9d.

Few tenants pay the full economic rent of the houses that they occupy, for if they live in a council house they are helped by substantial subsidies paid both by the Central Government and by the Local Authority, and if they live in a privately owned house they are protected by the Rent and Mortgage Interest Restrictions Acts, 1920 to 1939. We discuss below the effect of the subsidies, and the system of rent control established by the Acts named.

Housing subsidies

From 1919 onwards, houses built by Local Authorities in the United Kingdom have been eligible for subsidies from the Central Government and the Local Authority, in order that they may be let to the tenants at rents substantially lower than would otherwise be necessary. The total of the subsidies, and the proportions borne respectively by the two subsidising authorities, has varied from time to time. On every house built by the Local Authority since the Second World War, there is a subsidy averaging £22 a year — £16 10s. from the national exchequer and £5 10s. from the rates. Altogether in York in 1950, subsidies were being paid in respect of 6,212 council houses. The total received from the Exchequer was £61,062 and from the rates £26,765.

The subsidy paid on any particular house depends upon the Act of Parliament authorising the payment. Not only the amount of the subsidy, but also the proportions paid respectively by the Exchequer and the Local Authority, were varied by Parliament several times between 1919 and 1946. At the time of our survey, the average subsidy on the 6,212 council houses in York was £14 2s. 9d. per house, made up of £9 16s. 7d. from the Exchequer and £4 6s. 2d. from the ratepayer.

Rent control

Subject to certain exceptions, of which the chief are mentioned below, the Rent and Mortgage Interest Restrictions Acts apply to all dwelling houses of which in April 1939 the rateable value did not exceed £75 (or £100 if the house is in London).

The main types of houses exempted from the provisions of the Acts are all houses provided by a Local Government Authority, and houses let at a rent that is less than two-thirds the rateable value.

Although the application of the law to controlled houses differs according to whether they were first subject to control before or after 1939 (in which year the scope of the Acts was widened), it is sufficient for our purpose to say that the effect of the Acts is broadly to freeze the rent of a house at that in force at the time the house was first controlled, except that certain increases are allowed if the landlord has effected necessary structural improvements, or if he has had to pay increased rates in respect of the house.

The scope of the Acts is now such that every working-class house in York (except council houses which, as as stated above, are exempted), and most middle-class houses, unless they are occupied by the owners, are subject to rent control.

Since there is no free market in rented houses, it is difficult to know how great a financial benefit rent control is to tenants. It is, however, very considerable, and may well be as much as 10s. a week for a four-roomed house and 15s. to 18s. for one with six rooms. These benefits constitute another form of subsidy, the cost of which is borne neither by the Exchequer nor by the ratepayers as a whole, but by the individuals who own the houses.

The effect of rent control when seen from the point of view of the owner of the property is well illustrated by the case of a citizen of York who is well known to us. He owns a four-roomed house which has been let for a great many years at a rent of 7s. per week. After providing for all the necessary outgoings, including only such repairs as are essential to keep the structure in reasonable condition, the owner's net receipts from his property in 1950 were 1s. 8d. As the house becomes older, and the structure deteriorates more quickly, the owner's negligible profit will almost certainly turn into an annual loss. Having regard to the fact that existing tenants have security of tenure unless alternative accommodation is found for them, it is no exaggeration to say that the owners of such houses could not even give them away.

Sharing houses

We turn now to consider briefly certain sociological matters concerning housing, and first the question of two families sharing one house. The following table shows for each of the Classes 'A' to 'E' how many working-class families in York are sharing their house with another working-class family:

Class	Number of families sharing houses	% of families in the class
'A'	18	22.2
'B'	—	—
'C'	936	26.6
'D'	792	25.2
'E'	2,412	22.7
Total Classes 'A' to 'E'	4,158	22.9

The foregoing table includes only cases where two separate families inhabit one house; it does not, for example, include cases where an elderly parent is living with married children.

Save in a few cases the sharing of a house is not due to financial stringency, but to the inability of one of the families to obtain a house of their own. Whatever the disadvantages and discomforts of sharing a house, it is economical, and if all the families that are now sharing houses were provided with one of their own, a great many of them would drop from Classes 'D' and 'E' into a lower class, and not a few now in Class 'C' could not afford to have a house of their own at all without dropping into poverty.

Lodgers

The following table shows the number of families in Classes 'A' to 'E' where there are lodgers who have a bedroom, or sometimes only a bed, of their own, but who otherwise live with the family:

Class	Number of families having one or more lodgers
'A'	—
'B'	9
'C'	144
'D'	162
'E'	675

Overcrowding

With 22.9% of working-class families sharing houses it would be logical to expect a substantial degree of overcrowding, but in fact this is not the case. When B. S. Rowntree made his second survey of York in 1936, he examined the question of overcrowding by applying in turn each of seven different standards.* Because we have no information, as he had, of the size of rooms in individual houses, we have been able to apply only four of his seven standards. Our standards are:

(1) More than two persons to a room.

(2) The standards laid down in the Housing Act, 1935, under which a house is overcrowded if the number of persons exceeds:

      2   in a one-roomed house
      3   in a two-roomed house
      5   in a three-roomed house
      $7\frac{1}{2}$ in a four-roomed house
      10   in a five-roomed house
      12   in a six-roomed house

(3) B. S. Rowntree's "Standard A", which regards a house as overcrowded if there are more than $2\frac{1}{2}$ persons per room, with the exception of one room used for living purposes. This standard allows for the separation of the sexes at the age of 10 years, and it is assumed that the husband and wife occupy the same room.

(4) B. S. Rowntree's "Standard B", which is the same as his "Standard A", except that it does not assume that the husband and wife occupy the same room.

* "Poverty and Progress", p. 265, *et seq.*

In calculating the number of persons in each of the four standards, children from 1 year to 10 years are counted as one-half, and children under 1 year are disregarded. Where houses are shared by two families it is assumed that the families cannot be mixed in any way for sleeping arrangements.

According to the three least stringent of the foregoing standards, namely to those numbered (1), (2), and (4) above, there is now no overcrowding among the working classes of York. In 1936 B. S. Rowntree found that 1.7%, 1.9%, and 5.3% respectively of families were overcrowded according to these standards.

According to the most stringent of our four standards, namely B. S. Rowntree's Standard A, numbered (3) above, we found eighty-one families, comprising 612 persons (less than one-half of 1% of the working-class families), were overcrowded. The corresponding figures for 1936 were 1,106 families (6.8%) comprising 5,526 persons.

We do not suggest that these figures show that everybody now has adequate accommodation. On the contrary, many rooms are dark and small, particularly in the houses already scheduled for demolition as soon as slum clearance work can start again. But the fact remains that substantial progress has been made since 1936, despite the interruption of the war years, and this reflects great credit on those who have been responsible for the conduct of local government in York during the last fifteen years.

CHAPTER ELEVEN

HEIGHTS AND WEIGHTS OF SCHOOL CHILDREN

It had been our original intention to devote a chapter of this book to vital statistics and to ascertain the extent to which birth and death rates, and the infant mortality rate, varied in the five Classes 'A' to 'E'. To this end, we obtained from the Medical Officer of Health information concerning vital statistics in the city, and lists of all the persons who died, or were born, in York in the years 1949 and 1950. When we came to interpret the information, we were at once faced with a difficulty. Our 11% sample of the working-class families of York comprised 6,984 persons. The birth, death, and infant mortality rates in the city were respectively 17.3, 12.5, and 21.4 per thousand, so that we could only expect to be able to trace 121 births and 87 deaths (including those of infants) in any one year among the families whose economic circumstances are recorded on our schedules. The actual situation was even more difficult, for it often happens that a death, particularly if it is that of a householder or his wife, causes a family to split up so that it becomes difficult to trace their whereabouts and their circumstances. These facts so far reduced the number of families in which we could trace a death or birth, that we were left with numbers too small for any reliable conclusions to be based upon them. We were thus obliged to abandon the idea of examining whether vital statistics varied according to economic circumstances.

We wish to make clear that this does not in any way cast doubt upon the validity of our calculations in the preceding chapters. As we mentioned in Chapter 1, B. S. Rowntree, in the supplementary chapter of his book "Poverty and Progress", showed the degree of reliability of statistical samples of various sizes. Our sample—11%—is more than sufficient to give a reliable picture in those matters with which we have dealt in Chapters 3 to 10. It broke down in the matter of vital statistics only because death and birth are such exceptional circumstances that in any year they occur only to a few individuals out of every thousand.

Although unable to say anything about vital statistics, we have been able to examine the relation between health and economic circumstances in the case of school children. With the help of the Medical Officer of Health and the School Medical Officer of Health, we have been able to obtain the heights and weights of a large majority of the children of both sexes whose names appeared on our schedules. We were also able to obtain the heights and weights of a substantial number of middle-class and upper middle-class children attending private schools. We called these latter children Class 'X', and we give below a series of tables comparing the heights and weights of children of the same ages in Classes 'C', 'D', 'E', and 'X', and also show some comparisons between 1950 and corresponding figures for B.S. Rowntree's survey in 1936.*

* The number of children in Classes 'A' and 'B' is now too small for it to be possible to include average figures in the tables, but the few children in these classes for whom we have measurements are without exception slightly shorter and lighter than children of the same age and sex in Class 'C'.

HEIGHTS OF SCHOOL CHILDREN

Age	*Girls' heights*				*Boys' heights*			
	Class 'C'	*Class 'D'*	*Class 'E'*	*Class 'X'*	*Class 'C'*	*Class 'D'*	*Class 'E'*	*Class 'X'*
Years	*Inches*	*Inches*	*Inches*	*Inches*	*Inches*	*Inches*	*Inches*	*Inches*
4	40½	41¼	40¾	42¾	41¼	42	41	42½
5	42½	43¼	44¼	43¾	44	44	45	46¼
6	45	46½	46¼	47	46	46¼	46¾	47¼
7	48	48	48½	49½	47¼	48	48½	48½
8	49¼	49	49½	51	50	50½	50	—
9	51½	51¼	51	53¼	51¾	50½	53	53¼
10	53¼	53¼	54½	55	52¾	52½	55	55¾
11	55¼	55½	56	57¾	55½	55	56½	56¾
12	57	57	58½	59¾	57	58	58½	59½
13	60	61¼	61¾	61¾	59	60	61¾	62¼
14	62	62	62	63¼	61¼	61¼	62	64
15	62¾	63	63	63¾	62¾	64	64	64¾
Combined average	52¼	52½	53	54	52¼	52¾	53½	54½

WEIGHTS OF SCHOOL CHILDREN

Age	*Girls' weights*				*Boys' weights*			
	Class 'C'	*Class 'D'*	*Class 'E'*	*Class 'X'*	*Class 'C'*	*Class 'D'*	*Class 'E'*	*Class 'X'*
Years	*lb.*	*lb.*	*lb.*	*lb.*	*lb.*	*lb.*	*lb.*	*lb.*
4	37½	39¼	40½	43	40¼	41½	41¾	42½
5	41	42	44½	45½	43½	43½	45½	47¾
6	44½	49	48½	51¾	45½	49½	50¼	53½
7	53½	52¾	53¾	54	52½	53½	54½	54¾
8	55	54½	55½	62	58½	58¾	57¼	—
9	61¼	64½	63½	70	63½	60¼	64¾	64½
10	68¼	66¾	73½	76	67¼	68½	73½	75
11	68¾	76	80¾	85¼	77¼	76¾	80¼	78
12	77¼	80¾	84¾	92¾	81¼	88½	89	90¼
13	96	99	99¾	109¾	97	97	98¼	105½
14	110¾	112¾	116½	116½	100¾	101¼	111	113
15	119	118¼	118¾	121¼	108½	114	115¼	116½
Combined average	69¼	71¼	73¼	77½	69¾	71	73½	75

COMPARISON BETWEEN AVERAGE HEIGHTS OF CHILDREN IN 1936 AND 1950

	Girls				Boys			
	Class 'C'	Class 'D'	Class 'E'	Class 'X'	Class 'C'	Class 'D'	Class 'E'	Class 'X'
	Inches	Inches	Inches	Inches	Inches	Inches	Inches	Inches
1936	52	$52\frac{1}{2}$		$53\frac{1}{2}$	$51\frac{3}{4}$	$52\frac{1}{2}$		54
1950	$52\frac{1}{4}$	$52\frac{1}{2}$	53	54	$52\frac{1}{4}$	$52\frac{3}{4}$	$53\frac{1}{2}$	$54\frac{1}{2}$

COMPARISON BETWEEN AVERAGE WEIGHTS OF CHILDREN IN 1936 AND 1950

	Girls				Boys			
	Class 'C'	Class 'D'	Class 'E'	Class 'X'	Class 'C'	Class 'D'	Class 'E'	Class 'X'
	lb.	lb.	lb.	lb.	lb.	lb.	lb.	lb.
1936	68	$69\frac{1}{2}$		76	$66\frac{1}{4}$	70		$73\frac{1}{2}$
1950	$69\frac{1}{4}$	$71\frac{1}{4}$	$73\frac{1}{4}$	$77\frac{1}{2}$	$69\frac{3}{4}$	71	$73\frac{1}{2}$	75

The conclusions to be drawn from the foregoing tables are twofold. First, that on the average, children in all classes, including Class 'X', are taller and heavier than children of corresponding ages were in 1936. Second, that although differences in height and weight between children in one class and those in the next higher class have been reduced, it still remains true that on the average children in any of our Classes 'A' to 'E' are taller and heavier than children in any lower class, and that children in Class 'X' are, on the average, taller and heavier than those in Class 'E'.

A P N

NUTRITIVE VAL

	Quantity	Outlay		Calories	Protein
		s.	d.		gramme
All meat	6 lb. 0 oz.	6	7	6,336	403.2
Liver	1 lb. 0 oz.	1	6	640	76.8.
Beef sausages ..	1 lb. 0 oz.	1	3	976	52.8.
Bacon	1 lb. 4 oz.	2	4¾	2,580	44.0
Cheese	10 oz.		8¾	1,170	71.0.
Fresh milk ..	14 pints	5	10	4,760	252.0.
Herrings	1 lb. 8 oz.	1	0	888	72.0.
Kippers	1 lb. 0 oz.	1	0	592	51.2.
Sugar	3 lb. 2 oz.	1	3½	5,400	—
Potatoes	14 lb. 0 oz.	1	6½	3,584	89.6
Bread	23 lb. 8 oz.	6	2¼	26,696	902.4
Oatmeal	2 lb. 0 oz.	1	0	3,552	108.8
Margarine ..	2 lb. 8 oz.	2	1	8,720	—
Cooking fat ..	10 oz.		7½	2,530	—
Flour	1 lb. 4 oz.		4	1,980	66.0
Jam	1 lb. 0 oz.	1	2	1,136	1.6
Treacle	1 lb. 0 oz.		10	1,296	1.6
Cocoa	4 oz.		8½	500	23.2
Rice, Sago, and Barley	1 lb. 0 oz.		8¾	1,568	22.4
Peas and Lentils..	1 lb. 4 oz.	1	1¼	1,660	138.0
Dates	8 oz.		5¼	536	4.8
Swedes	6 lb. 0 oz.	1	3	384	19.2
Onions	4 lb. 8 oz.	1	10½	432	21.6
Apples	4 lb. 0 oz.	1	8	512	6.4
Egg	1 egg		3½	78	6.2.
Extra vegs. and fruit‡	—	1	6	322	27.2
Tea	8 oz.	1	8		
Extras	—		9		
		47	4	78,828	1,029.2.
					1,432.8

* International Units.
† Animal protein.
‡ Say, cabbage 2 lb. 8 oz., carrots 1 lb., and one large orange 6 oz.

)IX

THE DIETARY

alcium	Iron	Vitamin A	Vitamin B	Vitamin C	Vitamin C after deduction for loss in cooking
mgs.	mgs.	I.U.*	I.U.	I.U.	I.U.
288.0	86.4	1,248	2,496	—	
48.0	62.4	68,160	1,824	—	
144.0	9.6	48	688	—	
60.0	6.0	—	2,200	—	
300.0	2.0	3,690	90	—	
520.0	8.4	8,400	3,640	84.0	84
432.0	7.2	672	48	—	
320.0	4.8	496	32	—	
—	—	—	—	—	
448.0	22.4	—	5,824	1,568.0	784
016.0	188.0	—	19,928	—	
512.0	38.4	—	4,096	—	
40.0	4.0	22,720	—	—	
—	—	—	—	—	
440.0	14.0	—	1,700	—	
48.0	—	32	16	—	
112.0	6.4	—	—	—	
56.0	16.4	56	136	—	
36.8	3.2	—	304	—	
280.0	34.0	240	2,560	—	
148.8	4.0	80	—	—	
960.0	9.6	—	672	672.0	336
576.0	7.2	—	576	216.0	108
64.0	6.4	192	640	64.0	32
30.0	1.3	500	74	—	
750.0	10.2	25,756	920	664.0	368
,629.6	552.3	132,290	48,464	3,268.0	1,712

INDEX

A